Also by Ignatius Chithelen

Six Degrees of Education
From Teaching in Mumbai to Investment Research in New York

PASSAGE FROM INDIA TO AMERICA

A Note About the Author

Ignatius Chithelen is manager of Banyan Tree Capital in New York. Earlier he was an analyst and fund manager at First Eagle (SoGen) funds. A former reporter at *Forbes,* he has written for *Knowledge@Wharton, The New York Times* and *Barron's*. He co-founded Silley Circuits, a business network in New York City. Earlier in Mumbai, he was an assistant editor at the *Economic & Political Weekly,* taught Political Science at Khalsa College and science and math at Greenlawns High School. A Chartered Financial Analyst, he has a BA in philosophy and a MA in political science from Mumbai University, an M.Phil. in development economics from the Centre for Development Studies, India, and an M.S. in Journalism from Columbia University in New York.

PASSAGE FROM INDIA
TO AMERICA

Billionaire Engineers, Extremist Politics and Advantage to Canada and China

IGNATIUS CHITHELEN

Bryant Park Publishers

Library of Congress Cataloging-in-Publications Data
Names: Chithelen, Ignatius - author
Title: Passage from India to America: / Ignatius Chithelen
Description: First Edition./ New York: Bryant Park Publishers, 2018.
Identifiers: Library of Congress Cataloging Number: 2018900502
ISBN: 978-0-9974703-5-2 (hardback)
ISBN: 978-0-9974703-7-6 (paperback)
ISBN: 978-0-9974703-6-9 (e-book)

Subjects: LCSH: America - Entrepreneurs – Indians. / America - Engineers – Indians. /
America – Technology – Entrepreneurs. / America – Immigrants – India. / America -
Racism – Indians. / India – Technology - Entrepreneurs. / India - Education – Engineers.
/ India – Development – Capital. / India – Business - Beef. / India - Politics – Hindu
Extremists. / India - Politics – Caste Quotas.
BISAC: **BUSINESS & ECONOMICS** / Industries / Computers &
Information Technology I **POLITICAL SCIENCE** / Political Ideologies /
Radicalism I **RELIGION** / Religious Intolerance, Persecution & Conflict
LC record available at https://lccn.loc.gov/2018900502

Cover design by Visakh Menon
Typeface: Minion, produced by Adobe Corp; designed by Robert Slimbach

For Sanjoy Ghose (1959-1997)

Who lost his life working for "a harmonious, inclusive India empowered by knowledge"

Sanjoy was a gentle, soft spoken, generous and inspiring college friend from Mumbai. A social worker, he founded and led several initiatives to provide education and job skills for the less fortunate in rural India. He had a degree in management as well as advanced degrees from Oxford and Johns Hopkins universities. His promising life was cut short at age 37 by members of a violent ultra-nationalist group in Assam. They stuffed his body into a bag and dumped it in the Brahmaputra river. Like Sanjoy, many are courageously working to bring about helpful changes.

Rabindranath Tagore's Vision of a Free India

Where the mind is without fear
and the head is held high;
Where knowledge is free;
Where the world has not been
broken up into fragments
by narrow domestic walls; ...
Where the clear stream of reason
has not lost its way into the
dreary desert sand of dead habit; ...
Into that heaven of freedom,
my Father, let my country awake.

From *The Gitanjali*, 1913

CONTENTS

:

Introduction

AMERICAN JOBS. INDIAN COWS

India is the world's leading source of emigrant labor. Over 20 million Indians work as engineers, doctors, scientists, managers and other professionals in the U.S., Canada and Australia and as technicians, carpenters, nurses and teachers in Saudi Arabia, Kuwait, Malaysia and other countries. They are hence unlike the 12 million Mexicans, the second largest emigrant group, many of whom work in unskilled jobs in the U.S. There are over four million Indians in the U.S., over a million in Canada and 400,000 in Australia, mostly professionals; also 1.5 million in Great Britain.

Indian emigrants have had the most success in America. Three out of four Indian adults in the U.S. have a college degree. The median annual household income of Indians in America is over $100,000, a third higher than that of other Asians and 75% greater than that of American households, according to a Pew Research Center report. Indians have founded thousands of companies in America, mostly in computer and other high technology businesses. Several hundred thousand occupy middle and high-ranking managerial jobs, including as chief executives of Microsoft, Google, PepsiCo and over 20 other major companies. Many of the founders, CEOs and senior managers have a net worth of over a $100 million. In 2018, there were nine Indian-Americans on the *Forbes* list of global billionaires, including seven engineers -

four of them from the world renowned Indian Institutes of Technology (IIT) - and two science graduates.

These achievements raise several questions. What are the reasons for the success of Indians in America? What is their contribution to America? Will their children be equally successful, given the growing competition among Asian Americans for admissions to the top American colleges? How does India produce world-class engineers, managers, doctors and scientists? What do the emigrants owe India for their heavily subsidized education?

The first jobs Indian emigrants find in America are with companies sponsoring them for H-1B skilled worker visas. During the 2016 American Presidential campaign, Donald Trump and his advisers attacked the visa program for "displacing American jobs." In October 2016, a few weeks before the election, Trump spoke to a crowd of Indians in New Jersey. The rally, organized by the Republican Hindu Coalition, attracted wide publicity in America due to Trump's anti-immigration stance.

Four months later, in a sad irony, a White gunman in Kansas shot dead Srinivas Kuchibhotla, assuming the Hindu engineer was an Iranian-Muslim. Since Trump's election, Indians in the U.S. face a sharp rise in racial attacks and racism, including in Silicon Valley, home to Indian-American billionaires. Indians face resentment not just from some Whites. Many Blacks and Hispanics see them as unfairly taking college seats as well as jobs and business contracts set aside for minorities. How will rising racism impact the prospects for Indians in America? Will the board of a company, especially one doing business with the U.S. government, promote an Indian to be its chief executive or even a senior executive? What can Indians do to counter the hate?

Meanwhile the opportunities for Indians to emigrate to America are shrinking due to cuts in the number of skilled worker, spousal, student training and entrepreneur visas. These cuts are part of President Trump and the Republican party's "Buy

American, Hire American" policies. They are also backed by several lawmakers from the Democratic Party. The reduction in skilled worker visas is hurting Tata Consultancy Services, Infosys, Wipro, Tech Mahindra and other information technology (IT) businesses based in India. These outsourcing companies are firing thousands of employees, including engineers and managers. This is the first major, sustained job losses in India's IT industry, which employs over four million in the country.

In 2017, a third of the graduating engineers from the Indian Institutes of Technology got no job offers. Will they, as well as India's top math, science and medical graduates, emigrate to Canada in search of better wages and careers? Or will Chinese companies, which are investing billions of dollars in India, be the major beneficiaries? Up until the 1970s, before China's accelerated economic growth, living standards in India and China were similarly poor. In 1991, the International Monetary Fund forced India to introduce economic reforms. At that time, Indian and Western economists and journalists predicted that India would be a tiger economy, growing as large as the dragon China within 20 years. The forecasts were wrong since, until recently, growth in India has been far slower than in China.

Following the election of Prime Minister Narendra Modi in 2014, forecasters again predicted that India's economy would boom and rival that of China. The major reason for such persistent optimism is the desire among Indians and Westerners to see India's economy, and hence its military strength, match up against China. Modi has initiated several good policies which, if implemented even partially, can help boost economic growth. But so far economic growth under his government is no different than it was during the previous Congress Party government.

India has attained good progress in telecommunications and renewable energy. Nearly a third of the 1.3 billion population have internet access through mobile phones. In energy, power from wind and solar systems account for 8% of the country's 330 Gigawatt installed capacity. Such growth was stimulated by policies of the Congress Party government, which have been expanded by Modi. Both businesses are driven by private companies earning good profits. Most other infrastructure, including roads, rail, shipping and storage and transport of food items need to be expanded and modernized. Many of these businesses are operated by loss making government-run companies. India's big banks, most of which are government-owned, are also losing money. Having accumulated $146 billion in bad loan losses, they are reluctant to lend, cutting funding for businesses. The losses widen the government's budget deficits, restricting its ability to fund infrastructure and major development projects. So Modi's government is eagerly seeking over $500 billion in foreign investments to meet his major long-term economic goals.

Four years into Modi's rule, there are few signs of India attracting major foreign investments, apart from in fast growing, profitable consumer businesses. Foreign investors are waiting to see if his policies deliver attractive, sustainable profits before they invest in infrastructure projects. In the 2000s, foreign companies - with America's Enron being a prominent one - abandoned projects of an equally ambitious economic plan pursued by the Congress Party government. They faced losses because policy reversals forced them to charge lower prices to appease businesses, farmers and consumers.

Western investors are also nervous over the rising Hindu extremism of Modi's Bharatiya Janata Party. Since Modi became Prime Minister, at least 23 Muslims and four low-caste Hindus have been lynched by Hindu mobs over unproven rumors that they killed cows or were selling or eating cow meat. Leaders of Modi's party and allied Hindu extremist parties encourage such lynch mobs, according to news reports. Civil rights groups, journalists, academics and others in India who criticize the lynching of

Muslims and low-castes have been assaulted and threatened by Hindu extremists.

The lynching and the attacks on civil liberties have alarmed influential Western business publications. For instance, *The Economist* carried several critical stories in a June 2017 issue, coinciding with Modi's visit to meet President Trump in Washington D.C. The cover of the issue was titled "Modi's India: The illusion of reform." Such criticism makes it more difficult for Modi to attract major investors from America and Europe.

Western journalists, executives and investors fear the potentially combustible mix of anger and frustration among the Muslims over the lynching and lack of education and job opportunities. It raises the risk of Islamic terrorist groups finding recruits among India's 180 million Muslims. India has the third largest number of Muslims, after Indonesia and Pakistan. So far, there have been isolated cases of Islamic terrorism, such as the bomb blasts on trains that killed over 200 in Mumbai in 2006.

Modi and most other leaders of his party are current or former members of the Rashtriya Swayamsewak Sangh (RSS) (National Volunteer Organization.) The RSS is a militant group with a long history of trying to transform India into a Hindu nation. In the 1930's, its leaders praised the racial policies of Adolf Hitler and the Nazis in Germany. One of them said, "If we Hindus grow stronger, in time Muslim friends … will have to play the part of German Jews." In 1948, a former RSS member shot and killed Mahatma Gandhi, saying that the leader was partial to the Muslims. Gandhi was a Hindu who led the non-violent struggle that won India its independence from British rule in 1947.

National parliamentary elections are due in 2019. In the last elections in 2014, Modi's party got just 31% of the votes. Most Hindus did not support it, especially low castes and some farmer castes. Yet it won a majority of seats in parliament because the opposing votes were splintered among several rival candidates.

Since 2014, results of state elections show that most Hindus continue to vote against Modi's party. Modi appears to be seeking re-election based on two major pledges: building a Hindu temple at the site of a mosque destroyed by Hindu extremists; and protecting cows, which are sacred to Hindus. The strategy is to inflame Hindu-Muslim tensions and get more Hindu votes. Will Modi's party win again? Can the opposition parties form a coalition and defeat Modi?

In the pages that follow, I seek answers to the questions raised. In addition, I discuss the grave risks for Indians taking on bank loans to study at American universities; Canada's pro-immigration policies; odds of admissions to India's top colleges; rise of engineer billionaires in India due to the rapid expansion of mobile internet access; the need for more entrepreneurs in India to create jobs; the caste and religion-based electoral politics in India; and past actions of Congress Party governments to suppress civil liberties and provoke religious clashes. I have studied and analyzed these issues as a graduate student and journalist, during the first half of my life in India, and as a journalist and investment analyst during the second half in America.

Ignatius Chithelen

June 2018. New York City.

Chapter 1

FROM COOLIES TO BILLIONAIRE
ENGINEERS IN AMERICA

The first major emigration of Indians to a foreign region occurred in the nineteenth century. British colonies faced a shortage of labor, following the official abolition of slavery in 1834. The British rulers of India shipped thousands of poor Indians, from famine-affected regions like Bihar, to their colonies in Africa and the Caribbean. Over half a million were sent to Mauritius and thousands more to South Africa, Jamaica, Guyana, Trinidad and Tobago and other regions. These workers were indentured labor or unfree contract servants, who worked mostly on sugar plantations.

In the 1970s, a second big wave of emigrants started leaving India for jobs in the Persian Gulf countries. They went to work in Saudi Arabia and the other Arab countries, whose economies were boosted by the sharp rise in crude oil prices. There are about seven million Indian office workers, masons, carpenters, welders, electricians and others working in the Persian Gulf countries, including about three million in the Kingdom of Saudi Arabia.

Major Contributors to the American Economy

From the late nineteenth century to World War 1, about 10,000 Indians emigrated to America and Canada. They were laborers, or coolies, who worked on farms and on building the railways in America. In 1965, President Lyndon Johnson signed the Immigration and Nationality Act. It abolished immigration quotas that favored Whites, mainly Europeans, which was in operation since the 1920's. After 1965, a few thousand Indian engineers, scientists and doctors got visas each year to pursue advanced studies and work in the U.S. During the 1980's, the number of Indian emigrants rose sharply. This was because more Indians were admitted for advanced degrees by U.S. universities, more Indian engineers were hired by the booming computer, information technology and other high technology businesses and since Indian Americans began sponsoring family members in India for permanent residency visas.

In the 1990's, companies in America hired several hundred thousand Indian engineers and math and science graduates to meet an acute shortage of information technology (IT) professionals. The shortage was due to booming demand from thousands of new internet companies as well as staff needed to tackle the Y2K problem. There were widespread fears that IT systems would crash and cripple operations, if they were not upgraded or replaced, when the date switched to the year 2000.

Three quarters of the roughly four million Indians in America have a college degree, according to a Pew Research Center report. Many are graduates of India's best universities and have advanced degrees from American universities. A third of them are engineers and math and science graduates, while many of the rest are doctors, scientists, managers and business owners.

Indians have the highest household income among ethnic groups in America. Their biggest impact is in the Silicon Valley area of California, home to about 200,000 Indians. They have founded thousands of companies, especially in the high technology field, creating hundreds of thousands of American jobs. Overall Indians contribute several hundred billion dollars to the American economy each year.

Power Behind Global Technological Companies

Indians in America have made several major technological discoveries: Amar Bose, inventor of noise-cancelling headphones and an innovative suspension system for cars; his son Vanu Bose, whose inventions enable multiple wireless communication networks, including cellphone systems, to use the same devices and who built cellular antenna systems that run on low energy and solar power; Ajay Bhatt who co-founded the USB standard for computers, while working for Intel; Vinod Dham, creator of Intel's Pentium Processor; Sabeer Bhatia co-founder of Hotmail, which was acquired by Microsoft; and K.R. Sridhar, an early pioneer in fuel-cell energy systems for renewable plants.

Several hundred thousand Indians work for American technology companies. In 2003, Bill Gates co-founder of Microsoft said that engineers from the Indian Institutes of Technology (IIT) have done "great things" for his company. "We've hired literally hundreds and hundreds of graduates just in the last two years...and we're doing our best to increase the number," he continued. Gates was speaking at an event celebrating the 50th anniversary of the founding of the IITs, in Cupertino, California. As at Microsoft, Indians provide critical technical and managerial skills at Cisco Systems, Intel, Google, Facebook and other American technology companies. They account for 20% or more of the engineers and math graduates working at these companies. Their work has enabled American companies to globally dominate the computer, software, internet, social media and other technology businesses.

Thousands of Indians have risen to senior managerial positions, including as chief executives. The CEO's include: Sundar Pichai at Google, whose parent company Alphabet is valued at

$770 billion; Satya Nadella at Microsoft, with a market value $650 billion; Shantanu Narayen at Adobe Systems, which sells software tools for digital publishing and media services, with a market value of $92 billion; Francisco D'Souza at Cognizant Technology, an IT services and consulting company, valued at $44 billion; and Sanjay Jha at Global Foundries, a computer chip maker, with 18,000 employees, owned by Mubadala, the investment fund of the government of Abu Dhabi. Sanjay Mehrotra is CEO of Micron Technology, a memory chip maker with a market value of $71 billion. He holds more than 70 patents. He has B.S. and M.S. degrees in electrical engineering and computer science from the University of California, Berkeley and an executive MBA from Stanford University.

Lucrative Financial Rewards

CEO's as well as senior executives of American companies get lucrative financial rewards through a combination of salary, bonus, stock options and grants. Several Indian American executives have a net worth exceeding $100 million. Jayshree Ullal is a billionaire and one of America's wealthiest female executives. Since 2008, she has been chief executive of Arista Networks, a computer networking company. In 2017, she sold well over $300 million of stock she owned in Arista Networks. She owns an additional $980 million of stock in the company. Earlier from 1993 to 2008, she was at Cisco Systems, a rival computer networking company. She has a B.S. in electrical engineering from San Francisco state university and a M.S. in engineering management from Santa Clara university. In 2018, Google CEO Sundar Pichai cashed in $380 million, following the vesting of stock options issued to him. He has several hundred million dollars in additional stock options which will vest in the future.

In 2017, Thomas Kurian earned $36 million as president of

product development at Oracle Corp. It's a software company with an enterprise value of $207 billion. Thomas was also paid $35 million in each of the previous two years. He joined Oracle in 1996. From 2000 to 2017, he was awarded 52.4 million shares and options in the company, much of which he sold. In 2017, he owned 11.5 million of Oracle stock and options, with a gross value of $600 million. Thomas is the twin brother of George Kurian, the CEO of NetApp, a $12 billion software company. George joined NetApp in 2011 as a senior vice president, from Cisco where he was a vice president. In 2017, George's compensation from NetApp totaled $9 million and he owned 308,000 shares and options with a gross value of $19 million.

Both brothers got a BA in electrical engineering from Princeton University and MBAs from Stanford. They graduated from St. Joseph's Boys High School in Bangalore, which was founded by Jesuit priests in 1858. Thomas left IIT Madras to study at Princeton. He is on the advisory council at Princeton and Stanford universities and was chair of the Silicon Valley chapter of the American Heart Association.

Neeraj Arora is vice president of business development at WhatsApp, the messaging app owned by Facebook. In 2011, after four years at Google, he left to join WhatsApp, then a small, growing business facing competition from major rivals. Facebook bought it in 2014 for $19 billion in stock, cash and deferred option payments. Arora reportedly owned 1% of WhatsApp, then valued at about $160 million.

Assuming he has not sold any of the Facebook stock he received from the sale, Arora's net worth ought to be over $360 million. Meanwhile he has accumulated options in Facebook which should be worth millions more. Earlier in 2000, he took a risky job at a start-up in Singapore, instead of working for Infosys, a major Indian IT company. This was the key to his subsequent success since he quickly learned how to make decisions, Arora told students at the Indian School of Business, Hyderabad, in 2014. He got his MBA from the school, after a degree in mechanical engineering from IIT Delhi. In 2015, Arora funded a scholarship at the business school to pay the total costs for one student, which is about $51,000.

Professionals turned Entrepreneurs

Since the 1980's, Indian professionals have used their technical and business knowledge to found several companies in America. According to a 2016 study by the National Foundation for American Policy, Indians started 14 of the 87 fast-growing private American companies, with a valuation of over $1 billion. This was twice as many than those set up by entrepreneurs from Canada and the United Kingdom. Syed Ali, one of the Indians, is founder and chief executive of Cavium. It designs, develops and markets semiconductor processors for IT networks. It has an enterprise value of $6.4 billion. Ali is a graduate in electrical engineering from Osmania University and an M.S. from the University of Michigan. Jahangir Mohammed founded cloud based services provider Jasper. In 2016, it was acquired by Cisco Systems for $1.4 billion. Mohammed is a graduate of the Coimbatore Institute of Technology, India, and has an M.S. from Concordia University in the U.S.

Francis deSouza co-founded two companies: IMlogic, which was acquired by Symantec, and Flash Communications, which was acquired by Microsoft. He is chief executive of Illumina, a $30 billion genome-based biotechnology company. In 2001, Dev Ittycheria founded BladeLogic, a software company. Seven years later it was sold to BMC Software for $900 million. He also founded Applica, a cloud-based software company. In 2017, Ittycheria was appointed CEO of MongoDB, a New York-based database platform that enables developers to improve the productivity of data and software. Mongo is a publicly listed company valued at $1.5 billion. Earlier Ittycheria was an investing partner at Greylock Partners, an American venture capital firm. He has an engineering degree from Rutgers University

Other company founders include Ragy Thomas of Sprinklr, a social media platform, valued at $1.8 billion in 2016. Thomas is a graduate in computer science from Pondicherry University, India, and has an MBA from New York University. In 2008, Divya Narendra founded SumZero in New York. It's a web service that tracks the performance of investment research reports uploaded by analysts and fund managers. Over 16,000 finance professionals around the globe have access to the reports.

Earlier Narendra and two others created a social network ConnectU, while studying at Harvard University. They sued fellow Harvard student Mark Zuckerberg, founder of Facebook, for alleged intellectual property infringement. The three co-founders of ConnectU reportedly got a $100 million cash and stock settlement from Zuckerberg. Facebook has a market value of about $535 billion. In 2011, *Social Network,* a movie based on the story, won three Oscar awards. Its global box office receipts are about $225 million. Narendra's character in the movie is played by Max Minghella. Narendra got a degree in applied mathematics from Harvard University and a joint MBA and law degree from Northwestern University.

Indian entrepreneurs realize that job security, as in a job for life, does not exist in America. Also, that it's OK to fail. If a start-up fails, as nine out of ten do, founders move on to apply the lessons learned to their next job or at another start-up. Apoorva Mehta failed at 20 businesses, including building a social network for lawyers, between leaving a job at Amazon in 2010 and co-founding Instacart in 2012. "After going through all these failures...I realized...I didn't care about lawyers," or the other products that failed, he told the *Los Angeles Times* in 2017. He started Instacart in

San Francisco since he loved to cook but could not get the groceries he wanted because he did not own a car. The company is valued at $3.4 billion and is funded by top American venture firms, including Sequoia Capital and Khosla Ventures. Born in India, Apoorva grew up in Canada, before emigrating to America.

Billionaire Engineers

The U.S. is unique in providing the freedom "...to be able to dream big dreams, the freedom to achieve purely based on merit rather than family background or previous history of wealth or social status," Romesh Wadhwani told *Forbes*. He is a serial entrepreneur, on the 2017 *Forbes* list of 400 wealthiest Americans, with an estimated net worth of $3.1 billion. The other Indian billionaires on the list include Rakesh Gangwal, co-founder of InterGlobe Aviation; Kavitark Ram Shriram of Sherpaloo Ventures; and Vinod Khosla of Khosla Ventures. "For most Indians in America, wealth is not inherited...For us to make it to the top, we have to use our knowhow to create great new technology products and build high-tech companies," Wadhwani told the *Economic Times*. In 1969, after an engineering degree from IIT, Bombay, he emigrated to the U.S. and got a Ph.D. at Carnegie Mellon University.

"I had no previous business experience whatsoever," Wadhwani told *Forbes*, speaking about his first start-up, an industrial controls company. As in his case, a striking aspect about most Indian professionals turned entrepreneurs in the U.S., is that they are not from business castes and families. Vinod Khosla grew up in an Indian army household with no business or technology connections. In 1982, after an MBA from Stanford, he co-founded Sun Microsystems, a pioneering vendor of computer workstations and Java and other software. Sun was bought by Oracle for $7.4 billion in 2010. An electrical engineer from IIT Delhi, Khosla got a

M.S. in biomedical engineering from Carnegie Mellon University.

Like all entrepreneurs, Indians are motivated by a business challenge as well as the desire to become rich. Till recently, the initial capital required to start most IT based businesses in the U.S. was a few thousand dollars. In 1980, Bharat Desai and Neerja Sethi started their IT services business in Troy, Michigan, with an investment of $2,000. Syntel, the company the husband and wife team started after leaving jobs at Tata Consultancy Services, had $30,000 in sales in its first year. In 2017, Syntel's sales reached $924 million. Desai, who owns 40 million shares of the public company, has a net worth of $1.3 billion. A graduate of IIT Bombay, he has an MBA from the University of Michigan. Sethi, who owns 30 million shares, has a net worth of $990 million. She has an M.S. in Computer Science from Oakland University, which is located in a suburb of Detroit.

Cloud Computing, Drones and other new Technologies

Several Indians in America are working in businesses based on fuel cells, cloud-based services, data analytics, electrical vehicles, artificial intelligence, drones and other advanced technologies. In 2001, K.R. Sridhar, a fuel cell energy pioneer, co-founded Bloom Energy. It provides on-site clean energy systems using electro-chemical processes. The research for the technology was based on a project that created air and energy from solar cells for the National Aviation and Space Agency. In 2008, Bloom's first commercial 100 Kilo Watt systems were shipped to Google. Valued at $3 billion, the private company has raised over $1 billion in funding, including from Kleiner, Perkins, a major venture fund. Sridhar is a graduate in mechanical engineering from the National Institute of Technology, in Trichy, India, and he has a Ph.D. from the University of Illinois.

In 2009, Dheeraj Pandey co-founded Nutanix, an operating

system software. It works across multiple hardware platforms and IT locations, including those based on private and public cloud-based networks. The system enables companies to centrally manage all their IT services such as Oracle and other software, data gathering and analytics and data protection and recovery. Nutanix' clients include AT&T, Toyota, the U.S. Army and Tata. The San Jose, California based company was listed on the stock market in 2016; it has a market value of $9.3 billion.

Pandey started his career in America in 1999 as a software developer for Trilogy, a small company based in Austin. He took up the job after getting an M.S. from the University of Texas, Austin, and having abandoned a Ph.D. in computer science. He then moved to Oracle and other companies where he met his team of co-founders. Pandey is a graduate of IIT Kanpur. Another co-founder of Nutanix is Ajeet Singh. Earlier, he was part of a team at Oracle developing cloud based products. An MBA from IIM Calcutta, Singh graduated at the top of his chemical engineering class at IIT, Kanpur. He left Nutanix to co-found Thoughtspot, which is creating a search and analytics platform using artificial intelligence. The president of Nutanix is Sudheesh Nair Vadakkedath. He has a diploma in engineering from the Government Polytechnic College in Palghat, India.

Mohit Aron was another co-founder of Nutanix, and its chief technology officer. In 2013, he left to found Cohesity since the other leaders of Nutanix did not want to pursue his business ideas. In 2017, he owned around 5% of Nutanix, then worth over $300 million, which was held in trusts for his children. Cohesity provides unified computer hardware and networking systems software. They allow users to consolidate all backups, files, objects, copies and analytics, providing greater data protection and ease of use. Such secondary data, which use up 80% of an enterprise's storage capacity, is held in a variety of systems that are fragmented, complex and inefficient. Cohesity's clients include businesses, the

University of California, Santa Barbara, as well as the U.S. Air Force, the Departments of Energy, Justice and several other American government agencies.

The start-up, valued at $500 million, has raised $160 million from Sequoia Capital and the venture arm of Alphabet, Google's parent. In 2003, Aron started working as an engineer at Google. He got stock options priced at $1.20; Google parent Alphabet's stock reached a high of $1,186 in 2018. Aron built on his earlier successes, telling *Business Insider* that he advises others to "make yourself financially secure first" and then take bigger and bigger risks. In 2000, he got a Ph.D. in computer science from Rice University, which is based in Houston. He is an engineering graduate of IIT Delhi.

George Mathew is chief executive of Kespry, based in Menlo Park, California. Images from its drones automate processes in several industries, including estimating the size of inventories at mines and calculating damage to homes and commercial buildings from hurricanes and other disasters. The company has raised $61 million in funding, including from the venture capital arms of Cisco Systems and Shell. Earlier Mathew was global vice president of business intelligence at software giant SAP and president of analytics software provider Alteryx. He has seven patents pending around aerial data precision. He has a B.S. in neurobiology from Cornell and an MBA from Duke. Jitender Aswani, head of products and analytics at Kespry, is an electrical engineer from IIT, Varanasi, and an MBA from the University of Chicago. Earlier, Aswani worked at Facebook and was a co-founder and head of technology of a start-up Datadolph.

In 2004, Mihir Shukla founded Automation Anywhere. Its systems help technology companies like Google, Cisco and LinkedIn as well as banks and other businesses reduce costs and improve productivity by automating work processes. Shukla earlier ran several companies. He has a degree in computer science from

MS university in Baroda, India.

From Software to Marijuana Oil

Several Indian professionals in the U.S. have set up enterprises which are not based on high technology. In 2015, Amol Sarva co-founded Knotel which provides flexible office space to companies with over 50 employees. It has 800,000 square feet of office space in New York, San Francisco and London. Knotel has raised $95 million in two rounds of funding, including from Bloomberg Beta, building owners and real estate services providers. Sarva founded Knotable, an app for teamwork, and co-founded Halo Neuroscience, a stimulation technology that boosts brain function. In 2007, he co-founded Peek, a global mass market smartphone service. It charged $30 a month for internet and email access. It raised $25 million in venture funds. In 2012, Peek was bought by Bharti SoftBank, which used it to expand its offerings of Hike services in India and elsewhere.

Sarva is on the board of Plethora, a provider of metals parts, and advisor to numerous companies including Fon, the world's largest Wi-Fi network, and Payfone, a mobile payments system. He is also an adviser to Work Market whose software enables finding, managing and paying freelancers and contractors. A funding round reportedly valued the company at $72 million. In 2018, it was acquired by ADP, a human resources and payroll services firm. ADP has a $56 billion market value.

Earlier in 2000, Sarva joined Virgin Mobile USA, part of the founding team of the business set up by British entrepreneur and billionaire Richard Branson. Through a family angel fund, Sarva has invested in over 50 start-ups ranging from food delivery and kids clothing to electric bikes and robots. A mentor to several start-ups, he teaches entrepreneurship at Columbia University. He has a B.S. from Columbia and a Ph.D. in cognitive science from

Stanford. He was a national debate champion while at Stuyvesant High School in New York, the leading public school in the city. One of Sarva's photographs is in the permanent collection of the Museum of Modern Art, New York, and he has done collaborative work on a painting which is in a collection at Syracuse University.

Nitin Khanna is in an unusual business for an IT engineer, namely extracting oil from marijuana. The sale and use of the weed was recently legalized in several states. In 2015, Khanna founded Cura Cannabis Solutions based in Portland, Oregon. It has operations in Oregon, California and Nevada. Cura's sells its oil in vaporizers with vanilla, watermelon, peppermint and other flavors, that is smoked by consumers. It also sells its oil to vendors who put it in food products. In 2017, Cura was the winner of *Dope Magazine's* best concentrate company. The company is forecast to reach $120 million in sales in 2018 and is valued at $200 million. Khanna is also the CEO of MergerTech, a firm that advises founders who want to sell their small technology companies. Earlier in 1998, Khanna founded Saber Corp. to provide IT solutions to state governments. He sold Saber in 2007 for $460 million. He worked at Oracle Corp., after an M.S. and B.S. in engineering from Purdue University.

In 2014, Vinit Bharara founded Some Spider Studios, which he and a partner funded. Based in New York and Los Angeles, it runs two web-based entertainment channels Scary Mommy and CAFÉ. Each month, they are viewed by over 100 million via social networks and an additional 20 million via the websites. Earlier in 2005, Bharara and a co-founder started Quidsi, a web-based retailer of baby diapers and other consumer goods. They got $60 million in venture funds. In 2011, they sold Quidsi to Amazon for $545 million. Bharara is a graduate of the University of Pennsylvania and got his law degree from Columbia University. He started his career at Cahill, Gordon and Reindel, a New York law firm. He is the younger brother of Preet Bharara, the former U.S.

Attorney in Southern New York.

In addition to professionals turned business owners, there are Indians from traditional business families who own a range of businesses in America: wholesale and retail diamond and jewelry; motels and hotels; retail stores selling candy, cigarettes and liquor and refueling gas stations.

Indian Venture Capitalists

Naval Ravikant is a venture capitalist and investor in social networking businesses. He grew up with little money in Delhi and New York and washed dishes to fund himself through Dartmouth College. He helped found successful websites epinions.com and vast.com and was an early investor in start-ups Uber, Twitter and Foursquare, which grew into multi-billion dollar companies. In 2010, Ravikant co-founded AngelList. The digital platform, which connects business founders to investors, has enabled over 1,200 start-ups to raise over $540 million in funding. "I'm always rooting for the small guy…call it growing up as a poor, fat, immigrant kid," he told *The New York Times*.

Like Ravikant, several Indian entrepreneurs in the U.S. have become major investors, including as venture capitalists. Vijay Pande, a general partner at Andreessen Horowitz, leads investments in the cross section of biology and computer science. Earlier, he co-founded Globavir Biosciences which discovered cures for Dengue fever and Ebola. Pande, a former professor at Stanford, is a Ph.D. in physics from MIT. Vinod Khosla of Khosla Ventures was a partner at Kleiner Perkins Caufield & Byers. His investment successes include Cerent, which was sold to Cisco Systems for $7 billion, and failures include Dynabook. Khosla has a net worth is $2.2 billion, according to *Forbes*.

Kavitark Ram Shriram was an early investor in Google and is a founding board member the company. Earlier in 1994, he joined Netscape which launched the first major internet browser. In 1998 Shriram joined Amazon, after it acquired Junglee, an online comparison site of which he was the president. In 2000, Shriram founded Sherpalo Ventures to invest in technology start-ups. His investments include Paperless Post, an online card and invitation service. He has a net worth of $2.1 billion, according to *Forbes*. A vice-chair of Stanford University's board of trustees, he has a degree in math from Madras University.

Promod Haque has invested in more than 70 companies, since joining Norwest Venture Partners in 1990. His investments include FireEye, a cybersecurity company, and Apigee, which was acquired by Google. Haque has helped create over $40 billion in exit values, by companies going public or being acquired. His net worth is estimated to be $800 million. He likes to spend time with his four grandkids, teaching them math and science to prepare for a technology-driven world, he told *Forbes*. In 1999, Ravi Mhatre founded Lightspeed Venture Partners. It was the lead investor in Nutanix which is valued at $11 billion. In 2018, MuleSoft, another Lightspeed investment, was acquired by Salesforce for $6.5 billion. AppDynamics, another of its companies, was acquired by Cisco in 2017 for $3.7 billion. Other investments include Natera, which provides prenatal genetic medical tests, worth $731 million and Goop, a beauty, fashion and wellness brand founded by actress Gwyneth Paltrow. Earlier Mhatre worked at Silicon Graphics, consulting firm Booz Allen and BDIS, a vendor of instruments for the biotech industry. He has a B.S. in electrical engineering, B.A. in economics and MBA from Stanford University. "Some people like to garden or golf," he says. "I'm interested in technology. If I could choose any career I wanted, I'd be doing what I do now."

Fortune 500 Chief Executives

Besides running major American technology companies,

33

Indians have also climbed to the top at several other companies. Many have attained senior positions at Wall Street and other financial firms. They include Ajit Jain, head of the insurance business at Berkshire Hathaway. Founded and run by Warren Buffett, it has a market value of $454 billion. Jain joined the company in 1986 and owns stock worth about $100 million. He has a degree from IIT Kharagpur and an MBA from Harvard. Since 2016, N.P. (Narv) Narvekar has been manager of Harvard University's $37 billion endowment. Earlier he managed Columbia University's endowment and was a managing director of equity derivatives at J.P.Morgan. He has an MBA from the University of Pennsylvania's Wharton School and is a degree from Haverford.

Cyrus Taraporevala is CEO of State Street Corporation, which manages funds and is provides custody and other back office services to other fund managers. The 225-year-old company has a market value of $36 billion. Taraporevala got a Bachelor's in Commerce from Bombay University and an MBA from Cornell. Vijay Advani is CEO of Nuveen, which manages $900 billion in investments. Earlier he was co-president of Franklin Templeton Investments and worked in emerging markets for the World Bank. He has a bachelor's degree from Bombay University and an MBA from the University of Massachusetts, Amherst.

In 2001, Victor Khosla founded Strategic Value Group. It manages $7.1 billion in funds, investing in distressed debt and private equity investments. Prior to starting his fund, Khosla ran a fund which invested in distressed debt in Japan, jointly with Moore Capital, a New York hedge fund. Earlier he was president of Cerberus, a New York hedge fund, and head of Merrill Lynch's distressed trading and corporate and real estate investment group. In 1989, he started his career at Citibank. Khosla has an MBA from the University of Chicago, an MA in economics from Vanderbilt and degree in commerce from Delhi University.

Vikram Pandit is co-founder of the Orogen group, a New

York investor in financial services companies. Earlier he was chief executive of Citicorp and head of investment banking at Morgan Stanley. He got a B.S. and M.S. in engineering and a Ph.D. in finance from Columbia University. Divesh Makan is founder of Iconiq Capital, an advisory and investment firm. It manages the wealth of Mark Zuckerberg, founder and CEO of Facebook, and other Silicon Valley billionaires.

Outside Wall Street, Indian American chief executives include Indra Nooyi of soft drinks and snacks vendor PepsiCo, with a market value of $160 billion; Dinesh Paliwal at Harman International, vendor of audio equipment, which was bought by Samsung for $8 billion in 2017; Rakesh Sachdev at Platform Specialty Products, a chemicals company, with a market value of $3 billion; Santosh Padki at Bare Foods, a vendor of baked snacks acquired by PepsiCo in 2018; Raju Narisetti at Gizmodo Media, which runs 17 digital media sites; and Anjali Sud at Vimeo, an online video sharing and distribution platform.

Advanced Research and Nobel Prizes

Indian Americans have achieved success in medicine, research, teaching, politics, music, comedy, writing, fashion and sports. Siddhartha Mukherjee is a cancer surgeon who teaches at Columbia University. His book, *The Emperor of All Maladies: A Biography of Cancer,* won a Pulitzer Prize and was made into a TV documentary. He is a Rhodes Scholar who studied at Oxford, Harvard and Stanford. Sanjay Gupta is a neuro-surgeon who teaches at the Emory University School of Medicine, Atlanta. He is the chief medical correspondent for CNN and winner of multiple Emmy awards, given to professionals in television. He got his medical degree from the University of Michigan.

Atul Gawande is a professor at Harvard Medical School and two times National Magazine Awards winner. His writings helped shape President Barack Obama's health care insurance policies. In 2018, he was appointed chief executive of an independent, non-profit employee health care company. It was formed by the retailer and technology company Amazon, J.P. Morgan Chase bank and Berkshire Hathaway, which runs insurance and other businesses. The three companies have a combined market value of $1.7 trillion. They launched the healthcare company to improve the quality and reduce the costs of healthcare for their employees. Once proven, its services are likely to be expanded to serve other companies and will bring about major changes to the healthcare business in America. Gawande got a B.A. from Stanford, an M.A. from Oxford as a Rhodes Scholar and a medical degree and Masters' in public health from Harvard.

In the field of research, in 1968 Har Gobind Khurana got the Nobel Prize in medicine for his work in the field of genetics. A Ph.D. from the University of Liverpool, he conducted studies in biology and chemistry at the University of Wisconsin and MIT. Born in Punjab, he became a U.S. citizen. In 1983, Subramanyan Chandrasekhar got the Nobel Prize in physics for his work in the astrophysics of stars. He got a Ph.D. from Cambridge and taught at the University of Chicago, where he guided over 50 Ph.D. students. NASA's premier Chandra x-ray astronomy observatory, located at Harvard university, is named after him. In 1998, Amartya Sen was awarded the Nobel Prize in economics for his work on welfare issues and poverty. A Ph.D. from Cambridge University, he is a professor at Harvard University.

In 2013, Raj Chetty was awarded the John Bates Clark medal by the American Economic Association. The medal recognizes achievements by an economist under age 40. Several past winners have gone on to win the Nobel Prize. A professor of economics at Stanford University, Chetty got a B.A. and Ph.D. from Harvard University. A year later, Manjul Bhargava won the Fields medal, the highest award in mathematics. Earlier, at age 28, he was hired by Princeton University making him the second youngest full professor in the history of the university. Bhargava told *Quanta Magazine* that Sanskrit poems and playing the tabla, an Indian percussion instrument, helped him solve math problems. He got a B.A. from Harvard and a Ph.D. from Princeton. In 2010, S.R. Srinivasa Varadhan was awarded the National Medal of Science by President Barack Obama. It is the highest honor given by the U.S. government to "scientists, engineers and inventors." A professor at New York University, Varadhan got a B.A. and M.A. in math from Madras University and a Ph.D. from the Indian Statistical Institute.

Several Indians head major universities and schools. Renu Khator is president of the University of Houston, which has about 36,000 students. She got a Ph.D. in political science and public administration from Purdue University. Rakesh Khurana is the dean of Harvard College. He is a graduate of Cornell and a Ph.D. from Harvard. Nitin Nohria is the dean of the Harvard Business School. He is a graduate of IIT Bombay and a Ph.D. from MIT's Sloan School of Business. Sunil Kumar is the chief academic officer of John Hopkins University and a former dean of the University of Chicago's Booth School of Business. He has a Ph.D. in electrical and computer engineering from the University of Illinois and an engineering degree from Mangalore University, India. Jamshed Bharucha is a fellow at Dartmouth College. Earlier he was head of Cooper Union, a top ranked college for architecture and engineering in New York city. The college did not charge students any fees till 2014. Bharucha studied violin at the Trinity College of Music, London, and got a M.S. in philosophy from Yale and a Ph.D. in psychology from Harvard University.

Thomas Zacharia is director of the U.S. government's Oak Ridge National Laboratory. It conducts advanced research in artificial intelligence, nuclear reactors, national security and other areas. It has an annual budget of over $1.4 billion. In 2018, working with IBM and Nvidia, the laboratory launched the world's fastest computer with a peak performance of 200 million billion calculations per second. The computer is faster than Chinese machines that held the title for five years. Zacharia has a B.S. in mechanical engineering from the National Institute of Technology, India, an M.S. from the University of Mississippi and a Ph.D. from Clarkson University, New York.

Republican and Democratic Politicians

Prominent Indian American politicians include Kamala Harris who was elected to the U.S. Senate from California in 2016. Earlier Harris was twice elected as California's attorney general. Before one election, Harris asked her aunt in Chennai, India, to pray and break coconuts at a Ganesha temple, according to *Rediff.Com*. Her mother Shyamala Gopalan, an immigrant from Chennai, was a breast cancer researcher. Her father, who came to the U.S. from Jamaica, taught economics at Stanford University. Harris' parents divorced when she was seven and she was brought up by her mother. Her website notes that she is the second African American woman senator and the first South Asian American senator in U.S. history. "Whether black or brown" Harris is a caring person, according to her aunt. Harris studied political science at Howard University and got a law degree from the University of California, Hastings College.

Rohit "Ro" Khanna, another Democrat, was elected to the U.S. Congress in 2016. He represents parts of the Silicon Valley area of California. Earlier he was an official in the Commerce Department under President Obama. He taught economics at Stanford University, studied economics at the University of Chicago and law at Yale. Khanna's inspiration for public service comes from his grandfather, who spent years in jail for participating in India's independence struggle against the British, according to his website.

In 2010, Nimrata "Nikki" Haley was elected Governor of South Carolina. A Republican, she is the U.S. ambassador to the United Nations, appointed by President Trump. Her first job at 13 was helping with the accounts at her parent's clothing store in a small town in North Carolina. Her parents are Sikhs. Some of her opponents attacked her for presenting herself as a Christian Methodist to win votes. Piyush "Bobby" Jindal is another Republican. He was twice elected to the U.S. Congress and as Governor of Louisiana. His family converted to Christianity, after moving to the U.S. from Punjab, India. Jindal reportedly sought to disassociate himself from his Indian heritage, especially during his elections campaigns.

Comedians and YouTube Stars

In the fields of arts and culture, Zubin Mehta was the musical director of the New York and Los Angeles Philharmonic Orchestras. Vijay Iyer, pianist and jazz musician, is a MacArthur Fellow. He has a Ph.D. from the University of California, Berkeley. Norah Jones' songs have won numerous Grammy awards. She is a daughter of Ravi Shankar, the noted Indian sitar player. "Sixth Sense," a film by M. Night Shyamalan, was nominated for an Oscar award. He is a graduate of New York University. Mindy Kaling, Vera Mindy Chokalingam, is a writer, actress and producer. From 2005 to 2012, she co-wrote 26 episodes of the TV serial "The Office." She is a graduate of Dartmouth College.

In 2017, Hasan Minhaj gained wide attention as host of the White House Correspondents' dinner, which was boycotted by President Trump. A comedian and actor, his *Homecoming King* is streaming on Netflix. He studied political science at the University of California, Davis. Aziz Ansari is creator of *Master of None*, the popular comedy show on Netflix which won an Emmy award. He studied business at New York University. He grew up in Columbia, South Carolina, where his father worked as a doctor. Lily Singh has 12 million subscribers for her 'Superwoman' videos on YouTube. She has expanded from comedy into acting, selling lipstick, promoting consumer products for a fee and writing a best-selling book *How to Be a Bawse: A Guide to Conquering Life.*

Since 1987, Ajai Singh "Sonny" Mehta has been editor-in-chief of Alfred. A. Knopf Publishers. His book authors have won 34 Pulitzer prizes. Sree Sreenivasan was the chief digital officer of the Metropolitan Museum in New York. Earlier he was the dean of students at Columbia University's school of journalism. He has a Master's degree from the school and a BA from St. Stephen's college Delhi. Bibhu Mohapatra is a fashion designer whose clothes are worn by Glenn Close, Jennifer Lopez and other Hollywood stars. He studied at the Fashion Institute of Technology, New York, after getting a M.S. in economics from Utah State University.

Vivek Ranadive is unique among Indian engineers and entrepreneurs. In 2013, he bought the Sacramento Kings, a National Basketball Association (NBA) team. Ranadive is leading an effort to attract $1 billion in investments to develop and revitalize downtown Sacramento, which is California's state capital. The plan includes a new 17,600 seat arena for the Kings, which is fully powered by solar energy. Earlier Ranadive owned a minority stake in the Golden State Warriors, an NBA team based in the Silicon Valley. In 2014, Ranadive reportedly earned $316 million when Tibco Software, a company he founded, was sold for $4.3 billion to a private equity firm. He is the founder of Bow Capital, a venture fund. He left Mumbai at age 16 and got his Bachelor's and Master's from MIT and an MBA from Harvard.

Ronnie Singh is another Indian making his mark in American sports, though also not on the field. He is head of marketing for NBA 2K, a digital video game. In 2017, over 8.5 million copies of the game were sold globally. The game, which sells for about $60, uses images and statistics of NBA players. Singh has over 360,000 Instagram and over 700,000 Twitter followers. He is the public face of NBA 2K and is known as Ronnie 2K. Earlier he worked at a law firm, after graduating in economics and law from the University of California, San Diego. NBA 2K is owned by Take-Two Interactive, a producer and distributor of video games, with a market value of $12.5 billion.

Sunil Gulati was president of the U.S. Soccer Federation from 2006 to 2018. He played an important role in popularizing the game in the U.S., improving the national team's performance in several world tournaments and established a strong financial condition for the sport's governing body. He teaches economics at Columbia University. Earlier, working in the World Bank's Young Professionals Program, Gulati served as the country economist for Moldova. At age five, he emigrated with his parents to the U.S., from Allahabad, India. Gulati is a graduate of Bucknell University and got an M.S. and M.Phil. in economics from Columbia.

Benefit of Unique Social Skills

Indian professionals have several traits in common with other highly-skilled foreigners working in America: graduates of top universities, good work habits and ambition. They also have a good command of English due to their English language-based education at schools and colleges in India. They know how to succeed with few resources, having studied at India's top government-run colleges, most of which lack adequate facilities and equipment. Indians are able to handle intense competition and work pressure. In 2016, for instance, less than 1% of 1.2 million applicants were admitted to the IIT's. These and other top engineering, science and medical colleges in India are located in isolated campuses. There students get used to long hours of study each day, for months at a stretch, with few distractions. When they emigrate to the U.S., they find it easy to work long hours in demanding jobs, including in small cities, where many of them start their careers.

In addition, Indians go through a unique social experience which makes it easier for them to manage people and win at office politics. Growing up in India, they have to work, collaborate, compete and play with fellow students from four major religions, four castes, 20 major linguistic and cultural groups and different economic backgrounds, while seeking good grades and trying to win at cricket and debates. "Diversity is often ingrained in the DNA of Indians," Soumitra Dutta, dean of the Cornell College of Business told *The Daily Mail*. Indian professionals in the U.S., as well as in other parts of the world, intuitively grasp the motivations, ambitions, skills, temperament, work habits and culture of the diverse Americans and foreigners they deal with. They are thus able to figure out how best to work with bosses, colleagues, junior staff, clients, suppliers, investors and others, to achieve their career and business goals.

Chapter 2

PRESIDENT TRUMP & DEMOCRATS
CUT SKILLED WORKER VISAS

During the 2000's and 2010's, thousands of information technology (IT) and other professionals, including Indians, lost their jobs at high technology and other companies in the U.S. This was due to the collapse in demand for IT staff, after the internet bubble burst in 2000. Also, following the recessions of 2001 and 2008-2009, companies in America were cutting costs through automation and outsourcing of jobs. Some of the outsourced jobs were sent to India and other countries. Many of the advanced jobs were transferred to foreigners in the U.S., working on temporary skilled worker H-1B visas. The foreign workers, who were hired by American technology businesses as well as outsourcing companies, were paid lower wages than the employees they displaced.

From 2001 to 2015, Indians accounted for half of all foreigners who were granted skilled worker visas, according to a Pew Research Center analysis. Nearly 900,000 Indians, mostly engineers and math and science graduates, were hired during that fifteen-year period. Their temporary work visas were sponsored by Infosys, Wipro, Tata Consultancy Services and other Indian outsourcing companies as well as by Cisco Systems, Microsoft, Google and other American companies. Many of the visas went to outsourcing companies. In 2016, for instance, their employees accounted for half of those applying for visas to work at the headquarters of PayPal Holdings, 43% at Microsoft, 29% at EBay, 25% at Google and 12% at Facebook, according to *Bloomberg.*

Fifteen Year Wait for Green Cards

Lobbyists for associations of American engineers and IT workers, the media and politicians criticize Indian outsourcing companies for displacing Americans with cheaper staff brought in from India. This criticism is unfair since it is the American companies who fire employees to cut costs and improve profits. The Indian companies are merely fulfilling the demand for less expensive skilled labor. If companies in America are forced to pay high wages to either Americans or foreigners, as President Trump wants, they will continue to sack employees by accelerating the use of automation and rapidly expanding operations in lower wage locations outside the U.S. Owners and managers of companies are constantly seeking ways to maximize profits.

In 2016, visa applications for 4,500 contract employees, to be hired by Infosys, Wipro and other outsourcing companies, listed the average annual salary would be about $90,000. These employees were to be placed at Cisco System's headquarters in the Silicon Valley, *Bloomberg* reported. In contrast, Cisco was going to pay an average annual salary of $120,000, to the 3,000 H-1B visa applicants, it directly sponsored to work in the same office complex. So in 2016, at just one of its office complexes, Cisco sought to reduce its wage costs by $135 million by sub-contracting work to Indian companies. During 2016 and the first half of 2017, Cisco cut 1,330 jobs at the office where the jobs were to be outsourced, according to *Bloomberg.*

Engineers and other IT staff from India are eager to work for outsourcing companies in America since the salary is several multiples of what they would earn in India. But they have to work long hours, irrespective of work conditions, or risk being fired and sent back to India. This is because temporary skilled worker visas are valid only as long as they continue to work for the employer who sponsored them. The employee can apply for a permanent resident visa, or green card, which frees them to take up any job in the U.S. But Indians have to wait for at least 15 years to qualify for a green card, while working for the same employer. This is because the demand for green cards far exceeds supply. In 2017, for instance, there were two million skilled workers and their families waiting for green cards while only 120,000 green cards are granted each year.

If an employee leaves to work for a different company, while awaiting a green card, their application gets pushed back to the end of the green card line. "Opponents of the H-1B visa rightfully claim that American workers...are effectively competing with bonded labor," Vivek Wadhwa wrote in *The Washington Post*. He is a professor at Carnegie Mellon University Engineering at Silicon Valley and an Indian-American. The solution, he says, is to allow an employee on a skilled visa to take up a job with a different employer, without having to file a fresh green card application. But American as well as Indian outsourcing companies will oppose such a measure since they will no longer have control over a cheap employee, Wadhwa notes. Meanwhile, Indians who work on temporary visas, and then return to India or move to another country, enrich America's social security system by several billion dollars each year. This is because social security payments are deducted from their pay when they work in the U.S. But they won't get any benefits when they retire, since they are not permanent residents or U.S. citizens.

Fewer Opportunities for Indians in America

The opportunities for Indian professionals to emigrate to

America peaked during the 2012-2016 second term of President Barack Obama. For instance, in 2016, there were a record 186,267 students from India in the U.S., according to the Institute of International Education (IIE.) Nearly 90% of Indian students in America enroll for Master's degrees, which vary from nine months to two-years in length. The total fees and costs for the degrees range from $60,000 to $200,000, depending on the length, courses, colleges and location. Such costs, being three to ten times the gross annual income of the top executives in India, far exceed the savings of most Indian families. So, to fund their children's education at American colleges, many parents take on bank loans by putting up their homes as collateral.

Prior to Trump's Presidency, Indian students with advanced engineering, technology, math and science degrees had a good chance of finding well-paying jobs in the U.S. on skilled worker visas. In a worst case scenario, most of them could get a job for 29 months, on practical training visas granted through the American universities from which they got their advanced degrees. Such jobs enabled them to pay down much of their debt for their advanced degrees in the U.S., while also enabling them to gain good job experience.

Due to Trump's "Buy American, Hire American" policies, fewer companies in America are hiring foreign graduates on practical training and skilled worker visas. Also, more applicants for both visas are being rejected by the Immigration and other government departments. And work visas issued to spouses of H-1B skilled visa holders are being cut. In February 2018, the U.S. Citizenship and Immigration Services, which administers the issuance of visas, incorporated Trump's agenda in its mission statement. The department now says that it "administers the nation's lawful immigration system...while protecting Americans, securing the homeland, and honoring our values." The statement reflects the Trump Administration's principles, including "protecting American workers," a spokesperson for the department told the media. The earlier mission of the federal government agency was to enable the fulfilment of "America's promise as a nation of immigrants...(and) promoting an awareness and understanding of citizenship."

Since Trump's election, the number of Indian and other foreign applicants to American universities is falling sharply. For the 2017-18 school year, about half of all American colleges saw an average drop of 20% in foreign applicants, according to a survey by the IIE. The drop is sharper at lesser known colleges, even for M.S. degrees in computer science and that too in popular regions like New York. Some of the programs at these colleges are seeing up to 90% declines in the number of foreign applicants. The major reasons are delays and denials of visas, hostile social and political climate and sharply reduced chances of finding jobs in America after graduation. In the case of Indians, some of them fear they will lose their family home to the banks since they may be unable to pay back the student loans.

Democrats Support Trump's Skilled Visa Cuts

The Trump Administration is expected to cut the number of H-1B skilled worker visas issued each year, to well below the 85,000 issued in previous years. It is also working on implementing new rules under which the visas will be given to those with "the highest skills and wages." In 2017, two Republican senators introduced the Raise Act, which is a bill to cut legal immigration by awarding points for age, education, salary and ability to speak English. President Trump supports the bill saying it will favor highly-skilled immigrants. But critics point out that the effect will be the opposite. Since 2000, 31 of the 78 American Nobel prize winners were immigrants, Akhila Satish wrote in *The Wall Street Journal*. Based on the bill's criteria, she noted, a quarter of the prize winners would not have been granted immigrant visas to the U.S. Satish is an Indian American and a former research scientist at the National Institutes of Health.

Several Democratic lawmakers support President Trump's restrictions on immigration of skilled workers. One proposed legislation seeks to specifically restrict visas for engineers and other highly-skilled workers from India. In 2017, the Democrats joined the Republicans in the House Judiciary Committee to unanimously push legislation that will make it harder for Indian companies to bring in foreigners on high-skilled temporary visas. The proposed laws will require outsourcing firms to pay workers over $135,000 a year, up from the current $60,000; stipulates that no worker be laid-off by the firm or the client for the entire length of the visa; charges higher fees for the visas; and authorizes investigation by the Labor Department.

Zoe Lofgren, a Democratic lawmaker, helped write the bill. She states on her website that the proposed legislation would "curtail abuse...which has allowed replacement of American workers by outsourcing companies with cheaper H-1B workers." Lofgren's Congressional district includes San Jose and other parts of the Silicon Valley. There are thousands of engineers and other employees at high technology companies who are voters in her district. Lofgren must have their support – including from some Indian voters - for her proposed law, since they seek to protect their jobs and salaries through cuts in issuance of skilled visas.

Colleges Oppose Trump's Visa Cuts

Unlike the politicians, many college officials are sharply critical of the new immigration policies, saying they will shrink the pipeline supplying skilled foreigners from American colleges to powering its technology and other businesses. MIT, Stanford, Carnegie Mellon and 13 other universities, including all eight Ivy

League colleges, have jointly taken legal actions opposing some of Trump's immigration policies. At MIT, 40% of graduate students and faculty are foreigners. A great many "stay in this country for life, repaying the American promise of freedom with their energy and their ideas," L. Rafael Reif, the president of MIT said in a statement. Graduates of MIT have started more than 30,000 companies in America, generating over $2 trillion in annual revenues. Trump's immigration restrictions prevent top American universities from attracting the best global talent. This will drastically hurt America's ability to compete against China in the latest technologies, says Reif. He emigrated from Venezuela to study for a Ph.D. in electrical engineering at Stanford.

"America was built on immigrants," notes Michael Moritz, of Sequoia Capital. "Today it's impossible to satisfy Silicon Valley's appetite for engineers and scientists with people born" in America. Founded in 1972, Sequoia is the leading American venture capital firm. Companies it backed include Apple, Google, Oracle, Airbnb, WhatsApp, Yahoo, LinkedIn and YouTube. Moritz, an emigrant from Great Britain, is one of the billionaires who has signed the Giving Pledge. In his letter making the pledge he states, "Harriet and I never expected to become members of the Giving Pledge group but since our wealth-like all fortunes-rests so heavily on the intelligence, work and contributions of others it seems only right that we voluntarily give most of it to causes that help improve the lives of people we do not know."

Chapter 3

INDIANS FACE RISING
RACISM IN AMERICA

Some Indian Americans voted for Donald Trump despite his opposition to immigration of high-skilled workers. The Republican Hindu Coalition "swung 25,000 Indian-American votes" for Donald Trump in the Presidential election. This claim was made by Shalabh "Shalli" Kumar, speaking to *Breitbart News Network* at Trump's victory party in New York, in November 2016. The coalition says it organized over 50 meetings to canvass support for Donald Trump in the key states of Florida, North Carolina and Ohio. It raised $1.5 million for the Trump campaign and Kumar and his wife donated $898,000. The coalition spent $400,000 on an advertisement, with Donald Trump speaking in Hindi: "Ab Ki Baar Trump Sarkaar." (This time, it will be Trump's government.) The ad, which started with a Diwali greeting, copied the slogan "Ab Ki Baar Modi Sarkaar," which Prime Minister Narendra Modi used in the 2014 national elections in India. Kumar is also a strong supporter of Modi.

Kumar founded the coalition in 2015 as "a collective voice of conservative Indian Americans, Free Enterprise, Fiscal Discipline, Family Values & Firm Foreign Policy." He is the founder of AVG Automation, near Chicago, which designs and manufactures electronic automation products, according to its website. In 1969, he emigrated from Punjab, India, to study at the Illinois Institute of Technology.

"Down with Trump" Slogans at Engineer's Funeral

In October 2016, a few weeks before the U.S. Presidential election, Donald Trump spoke to a rally of Indians in New Jersey, which was organized by Kumar's coalition. "The Indian and Hindu community will have a true friend in the White House, that I can guarantee...Generations of Indian and Hindu Americans have strengthened our country...your values, your hand work; education and enterprise have truly enriched our nation and we will be celebrating a Trump administration together," Trump said, according to the coalition website. The event attracted wide publicity in America since it was one of the few rallies of a minority group in support of Trump. Also, his senior advisers were criticizing U.S. visa programs for enabling foreign professionals, mostly Indians, to steal American jobs.

Four months later, Srinivas Kuchibhotla was killed in a racial attack at a bar in a Kansas City suburb. Adam Purinton shot Srinivas and his friend Alok Madasani, both 32-year-old engineers from India. According to news reports, the White gunman had earlier asked them about their immigration status: "Where are you from? Why are you in this country?" Srinivas is said to have replied "We are here legally. We are on H1-B (work visas for professionals.) We are from India." The gunman assumed Srinivas and his friend, both Hindus, were Iranian Muslims and called them "sand-niggers." He reportedly said, "We pay for your visas to be here. You need to get out of here! You don't belong here!"

"My son had gone there (to America) in search of a better future. What crime did he commit?" Srinivas' mother told *The Guardian*. She said she would not allow her younger son, who was in Hyderabad for his brother's funeral, to return to the U.S. The father of Madasani, Srinivas' friend who survived a bullet wound, told *The Hindustan Times*, "The situation seems to be pretty bad after Trump took over as the US President. I appeal to all the parents in India not to send their children to the US." Trump waited six days before condemning the killing. He referred to it as "last week's killing in Kansas City" and did not mention that the man killed was an Indian immigrant. Srinivas' funeral in Hyderabad, India's second largest IT center after Bangalore. It was attended by thousands, including engineers working for IT companies. Many of them shouted slogans and carried banners saying "Down with Trump" and "Down with Racism."

Abrupt End to a Promising Career

Srinivas was 6' 2", tall for an Indian. After a degree from the Jawaharlal Nehru Technological University in Hyderabad, India, he got a Master's in electrical engineering from the University of Texas, El Paso. He became an expert at coding in Python, an advanced software language. In 2007, upon graduation, Srinivas was hired by Rockwell Collins on a temporary skilled worker visa. He worked at the Cedar Rapids, Iowa head office of the aviation electronics company; its 2017 revenues were $6.8 billion. "As an engineer, he was smarter than I was—without a doubt," his American mentor at the company told *Wired*. Rockwell appointed Srinivas to handle relations between its Cedar Rapids office and its team in Hyderabad. His co-workers nominated him Engineer of the Year. Rod Larson, his former manager at Rockwell told the *Kansas City Star* that "He was well-liked...excellent in all categories...a low-maintenance employee and did whatever was asked of him."

In 2013, while still awaiting a permanent residency visa, Srinivas decided to take up a job in a larger city. He joined Garmin,

Rockwell's competitor, as a senior aviation systems engineer at its headquarters in Olathe, a Kansas City suburb. He and his wife bought a $300,000 four-bedroom house and were the first Indians on the residential block. Srinivas was determined to stay in America. "We came here to achieve and fulfill our dreams," his wife Dumala Sunayana writes in a Facebook post. She was also from Hyderabad and has a degree in engineering management from St. Cloud State University, Minnesota. Sunayana was worried for their safety and wanted them to return to India, especially following the rise in racial incidents since Trump began his election campaign. With a hug Srinivas "always assured me that if we think good, be good, then good will happen to us and that we will be safe," Sunayana writes.

Resentment over Success

Racism against Indians in North America has a long history. The Indians who emigrated in the late nineteenth and early twentieth centuries were considered an undesirable Asian group, notes Joan Jensen in her book *Passage from India: Asian Indian Immigrants in North America*. In 1923, the U.S. Supreme Court upheld a law that barred Indians from becoming American citizens. The court noted that the "high-caste Sikh of Aryan blood," who filed the case, did not meet the criteria of being a Caucasian White. Indians were banned from migrating to the U.S. as well as Canada. Many of them were stripped off their citizenship and sent back to India.

In the mid-1980s, Indians living in some blue-collar areas of New Jersey faced taunts and attacks from Hispanic, Black and White youths. Indian women were spat upon and trash, stones and obscenities were hurled at Indian homes and businesses. A group of White youths attacked a Govinda temple, destroying the furniture and taking away the idols. Several Indian small business owners in the area received repeated phone threats that they would be killed.

"We will go to any extreme to get Indians to move out of Jersey City. If I'm walking down the street and I see a Hindu and the setting is right, I will hit him or her," a group called Dotbusters, said in a letter, partially published by a local newspaper. The group, which claimed responsibility for the attacks on Indians, took its name from the bindi, or colored dots, worn by Indian women on their forehead. Indians settled in and set up businesses and bought houses in Jersey City, where real estate prices are cheaper than in neighboring New York City. Some residents, who grew up in the area, were upset at the new immigrants. They said that, unlike them, Indians were getting government grants and loans. As the Indians "...became more affluent... resentment grew among those left behind," Jersey City's mayor told *The New York Times.*

In 1987, Navroze Mody, a thirty-year-old Indian man, died after being brutally beaten by four Hispanic youths, one night on a street in Jersey City. Mody had been recently promoted as a manager at a financial company in New York City. A few days later Kaushal Saran, 28, was beaten into a coma, on a busy street corner, also in Jersey City. Saran, who survived, was a recent immigrant from India. He was a doctor, awaiting a license to practice medicine in America. Local Indian community leaders wanted the four co-defendants, who attacked Mody, to be prosecuted for racially motived murder. But, three of the four were sentenced on the lesser charge of "aggravated assault," leading to a maximum jail sentence of ten years. The fourth was convicted of simple assault.

"Coolies Stealing American Jobs"

In the early 2000's, following the collapse of the Internet bubble, some American IT professionals were upset at Indians for "stealing their jobs." Comments such as "I lost my job to a coolie in

Bangalore" were made anonymously on online chat rooms. Coolie is an insulting term, used by the British when they ruled India, to refer to low-paid, unskilled Indian laborers. Following more job losses, due to the 2008-2009 recession, there was fresh criticism of granting work visas for Indian professionals. The waves of job cuts also led to several thousand Indian IT and other professionals in the U.S. losing their high wage jobs, including to temporary skilled workers brought in by Indian outsourcing firms. Unemployed Indians without U.S. work visas, and some with visas, moved back to India or to other countries to find work.

Racists in America often assume that Indians are Muslims and Arabs. "In many instances, especially after 9/11, bias crimes against Hindus have been based on the perpetrator's mistaken belief that the victim is Muslim or Arab," noted a 2012 petition from the Hindu America Foundation, to the Federal Bureau of Investigation (FBI.) The foundation, which says it is an advocacy group for Hindus in America, wanted the FBI to expand hate crime investigations to cover attacks on Hindus.

On September 11, 2001 - referred to as 9/11 - 19 Arab terrorists used four commercial planes as weapons, killing 2,977 in the U.S., including by destroying the twin World Trade Center towers in New York City. In the first month, there were over 300 cases of violence and discrimination against Sikhs in America, according to the Sikh Coalition. Balbir Singh Sodhi, a Sikh migrant from India, was shot dead outside the gas station he owned in Arizona, by a White gunman who mistook him for an Arab. There is often violence and discrimination against Indians in the U.S., following major terrorist attacks in the world, like those in Kenya in 2013, in Paris in 2015 and London and Manchester in 2017.

White Extremists Attack Indians and other Minorities

Since Donald Trump's election campaign started in 2015,

racial hostility towards minorities is more open and widespread. In 2016, hate attacks on Muslims, African-Americans, Jews, Indians and other minorities rose sharply. African-American were the victims of half the 4,229 hate crimes based on race that year, according to the FBI. Jews were the victims of over half the 1,538 hate crimes based on religion, the federal agency stated. An editorial in *The Washington Post* commented that "…it's noteworthy that many of the groups against whom (hate) crimes rose by double digits were the focus of inflammatory rhetoric by Donald Trump over the course of his presidential campaign."

There are angry, unsubstantiated comments against Indians, including on websites of reputed publications. In 2017, for instance, following a story in the *The Washington Post* that 70% of H-1B skilled visas went to Indians, a person named Tom commented: "I've been in I.T. for over 30 years and know not of a single, not one, American that has ever been hired by an Indian company operating in the USA." The comments on right-wing sites are more extreme. In 2017, for instance, one reader of *Breitbart* commented, "…Indians have nice 800,000 dollar homes while the workers they replaced are lucky to live in trailers plus don't forget they use the free school system." *Breitbart* was once promoted as a "platform" for the alt-right, a small, far-right movement that seeks a Whites-only state and whose adherents are known for espousing racist, anti-Semitic and sexist points of view, according to *The Washington Post*. The website is very popular among those who support Trump supporters. It is funded by some very wealthy conservatives.

Trump supporters and White political extremists also attack the skilled worker visa programs, which enables Indians to find their first jobs in America. Steve Bannon said in an interview, when he was Trump's campaign manager, that the "progressive plutocrats in Silicon Valley" want unlimited ability to go around the world and bring people back to the United States. On another occasion, he said, "When two-thirds or three-quarters of the CEOs in Silicon Valley are from South Asia or from Asia, I think…" not finishing the sentence. Bannon was chairman of *Breitbart*, the right-wing website. In 2017, he served as chief strategist in the Trump administration.

Some racists use "Indian" as a code word for foreigners they dislike. In 2017, Katie McHugh, then a reporter for *Breitbart*, tweeted "there would be no deadly terror attacks in the U.K. if Muslims didn't live there." Pej Vahdat, a television actor, tweeted that McHugh was a" real moron." Katie McHugh responded to Vahdat with a tweet: "You're an Indian." Vahdat is an American of Iranian descent.

A New Reality for Indians in America

In the first ten days after Trump's election there were 867 incidents of harassment and intimidation of minorities in America, according to data gathered by the Southern Poverty Law Center (SPLC.) The daily reports of such hate crimes is typically in the single digits, the civil rights group noted. The incidents included swastikas at schools and colleges, racist taunts and physical assaults. They have occurred in regions with large Trump supporters in the South and Midwest as well as in liberal areas like New York City and Silicon Valley. Besides Indians and other Asians, Blacks, Hispanics, Jews and gays were among those attacked. The SPLC points out that there is a clear connection to Trump's campaign and election: over a third of the attackers referenced Trump's name, his slogans or remarks.

In February 2017, ten days after Srinivas was killed, a Sikh man was shot outside his home in Washington State. The White gunman, who wore a mask, told him to go back to his country. A month later, a White man set fire to an Indian owned convenience store in Florida, because, he reportedly said, he wanted to "run the

Arabs out of our country." In Palo Alto, an Indian high school student wrote that he was told three times in one week to "go back to your country." The town is the wealthy hub of Silicon Valley, home to the campus of Stanford University and the head offices of major American venture capital firms.

Indians in high profile public jobs face a rise in racist taunts. In 2017, Sunil Gulati said he will not stand for re-election as the president of the U.S. Soccer Federation. This was after he got much of the blame, including racist comments on social media and blogs, for America's failure to qualify for the 2018 World Cup soccer tournament. Indians serving in the Trump Administration are also not immune. In 2017, Nikki Haley told *CBSNEWS* that women who accuse President Trump of sexual assault should be given a hearing. "Women who accuse anyone should be heard...and they should be dealt with," Haley said. At least 16 women have accused Trump of sexual misconduct, *Newsweek* reported. Haley was appointed U.S. Ambassador to the United Nations by President Trump. News reports said that Trump was upset at Haley for her remarks. Several readers attacked Nikki Haley on right-wing news sites. One of them wrote on *Breitbart* "India, where Slavery, I mean the Caste System, is still in full operation today!! Go back to Calcutta, Nikki!!"

Speak in English, not an Indian Language

In 2017, 17 people were killed in America by young men associated with White extremist groups, according to a Southern Poverty Law Center (SPLC) report. During 2017, Trump's first year as President, he "reflected what white supremacist groups want to see: a country where racism is sanctioned by the highest office, immigrants are given the boot..." writes Heidi Beirich of the SPLC. There are over 600 hate groups in America that adhered to some form of white supremacist ideology. The SPLC also identified

273 armed militias; neo-Nazi groups grew to 121 in 2017, from 99 the previous year, the sharpest increase among hate groups. The numbers likely understate "the real level of hate in America because a growing number of extremists, particularly those who identify with the alt-right (neo-Nazis), operate mainly online and may not be formally affiliated with a hate group," the SPLC states. Trump's "radical views and bigotry may be energizing them in the same way he has invigorated hate groups," the report notes.

Following the killing of Srinivas, some Indian organizations in America advised their members to speak in English in public spaces and avoid getting into arguments with strangers. "Much as we love talking in our mother tongue, it can often be misconstrued. Please see if you can communicate in English in public places," advised the Telangana American Telugu Association. It's a group from the same linguistic background as Srinivas. A member of the group from Texas said the killing of Srinivas triggered panic among Indians.

Left unstated but implied in the group's advice is that Indians in America should go about their jobs, careers and business quietly, with their heads down. They are not to question or object to overt and hidden racial insults, even small ones like Whites cutting ahead at the check-out lines at a supermarket. "The desire for advancement often breeds an apolitical attitude among immigrants, a desire not to rock the boat, to be allowed to pass unnoticed..." Amitava Kumar wrote in *The New Yorker* in 2017, in an article titled "Being Indian in Trump's America." But today the Internet constantly delivers ugly reports and rumors throughout the day, and "with them a sense of nearly constant intimacy with violence." Amitava is not related to Shalabh Kumar, founder of the Republican Hindu Coalition. Amitava is a writer and journalist who teaches at Vassar College, outside New York City.

Cows on the Street in Kansas City

The rise in racism in America, since Trump's election victory, will likely take years to subside; and much longer, if he is re-elected in 2020. A year into his presidency, while Trump has made a farce of his economic pledges, his campaign promises of a race-based agenda "...have been more faithfully enacted...As the president continues to pursue a program that places the social and political hegemony of white Christians at its core, his supporters have shown few signs of abandoning him." notes Adam Serwer in *The Atlantic*. With the rise in racism, more Indians will likely move to metropolitan areas with a diverse population like New York, Silicon Valley, Los Angeles and Boston. In such regions, they may feel safer in larger numbers. But there they will face intense competition for jobs and their children will find it tougher to get into good schools and colleges.

In the past, many Indian professionals found their first jobs in smaller cities in America. They then worked their way up the career ladder to the bigger companies and cities. Srinivas started his career in Cedar Rapids, Iowa, with a metro population of 266,000. He then moved to a suburb of Kansas City, a region with a population of 2.1 million. In June 2017, four math or computer-related jobs remained open for every unemployed worker in the Kansas City region. The shortage in Kansas, and other small and mid-size cities, will only get worse with Trump's visa policies and rising racism. Discussing the shortage of skilled labor, Pam Whiting, a spokesperson for the local Chamber of Commerce, told *Wired* magazine "People think we have cows running up and down the street."

Chapter 4

UPPER CASTES PURSUE MINORITY
BUSINESS CONTRACTS & JOBS

While Indians face rising racism in America, some of them are opposing the admission of Blacks, Hispanics and other minorities to the top colleges. At the same time, some Indians seek jobs and business contracts reserved for minorities. The National Federation of Indian-American Associations, the American Society of Engineers of Indian Origin and two other Indian organizations are among 64 Asian American organizations which formed the Asian American Coalition for Education. In 2015, the coalition filed a complaint with the U.S. Department of Education and the Department of Justice stating that over the last two decades, "many Asian-American students who have almost perfect SAT (Scholastic Aptitude Test) scores, top 1% GPAs (grades,) plus significant awards or leadership positions in various extracurricular activities have been rejected by Harvard University and other Ivy League Colleges while similarly situated applicants of other races have been admitted."

Since 1980, Asians make up over 30% of students representing America in global high school competitions like the science, math and computing Olympiads. Yet, the complaint says, the number of Asian American students admitted to Harvard,

Princeton, Yale and other Ivy League and top colleges has stayed between 14% to 18%, despite the increasing number of qualified candidates. It added that the top colleges reject high-achieving Asian-American applicants in favor of less-qualified Black, Hispanic and White applicants.

White Conservatives use Asian American Complaint

The coalition apparently want more Asians to be admitted to the top colleges by reducing the number of Black and Hispanic admissions. Leaders of the Indian groups deny this saying they also oppose admissions of less qualified White applicants. "A white kid should not get preferred treatment at the expense of Asians and the general quota should be based solely on merit, " one of them told *IndiaWest*. Meanwhile the Asian American complaint is being used by White conservatives, including President Donald Trump, in pursuit of their own political agenda.

In 2014, the Students for Fair Admissions (SFFA,) filed lawsuits against a top private and a top public university seeking the abolition of racial preferences in college admissions. It's a conservative non-profit organization for "...students, parents and others who believe that racial classifications and preferences in college admissions are unfair, unnecessary and unconstitutional." The SFFA says that the "affirmative action battle has a new focus: Asian Americans." Its website lists "high-achieving" Asian students who did not get into the top colleges.

The SFFA's lawsuit against Harvard alleges that the university is "employing racially and ethnically discriminatory policies and procedures in administering the undergraduate admissions" which discriminates against Asian Americans and gives preferences to other racial minorities. The SFFA made similar allegations against the University of North Carolina, Chapel Hill, a state run university. It notes that in 2013, Harvard's Asian

American enrollment was 18 percent. At universities that admitted students based solely on exam results, the lawsuit argues, Asian Americans made up a third of the students at the Berkeley and Los Angeles campuses of the University of California and 43% at Caltech. The group refers to a 2009 Princeton study which found that Asian-Americans need SAT test scores 140 points higher than Whites, 270 points higher than Hispanics and 450 higher than Blacks to get into one of the top private colleges.

Trump Orders Harvard Investigation

The Democratic administration of President Barack Obama ignored the complaint of the Asian American groups. But in 2017, soon after Trump became president, his Republican administration used the complaint to launch an investigation into admissions at Harvard. Opposing the investigation, the university stated that it's admission process reviews "...many factors, consistent with the legal standards established by the U.S. Supreme Court." Students are not admitted solely based on grades and test scores. They "...must have the ability to work with people from different backgrounds, life experiences and perspectives," a spokesperson for Harvard stated. After the government said it will sue, the university agreed to give the Justice Department access to the records of past applicants. The U.S. Supreme Court will likely decide the fate of the Harvard investigation and the SFFA lawsuits.

The Harvard investigation is welcomed by conservative groups who say that many White students are not being admitted to the top colleges despite higher test scores, to accommodate Blacks and Hispanics with far lower scores. One of them is the Center for Equal Opportunity, run by Republican Roger Clegg a former official in President Ronald Reagan's administration. In a statement Clegg said the investigation is an "overdue development that the administration will be taking a hard look at schools that insist on weighing skin color and national origin in deciding who gets admitted…racial preferences harm many low-income Asians as well as whites."

Kim Forde-Mazrui, a University of Virginia law professor, told the *Los Angeles Times* that White conservative "leaders purported concern for discrimination against Asian Americans is politically opportunistic." The Trump Administration's use of the Asian American complaint to investigate Harvard, "…is primarily about conservative leaders protecting the privilege of access to society's resources and opportunities for certain white constituents…", he added. Opposing minority college admissions "is a convenient scapegoat for those who seek to pit minority groups against each other," says Daniel Golden wrote in an opinion piece published in *ProPublica*.

Asians Oppose Conservative Strategy

Most Indians and other Asian Americans oppose the complaint, the lawsuits and the investigation. A 2016 poll, sponsored by Asian Americans Advancing Justice, found that 64% of Asians supported affirmative action programs which help Blacks, Hispanics, women, and other minorities improve their chances of getting admission to colleges. Asian students experience racial bullying, slurs and profiling and "…studies show that colleges and universities that reach the highest levels of diversity have fewer incidents of racial hostility," the group says. A non-profit based in Washington D.C., the Justice group's mission is "to advance the civil and human rights for Asian Americans."

The Asian group has filed legal arguments backing Harvard's admission policies. It notes that "a commonly held myth is that Asian American applicants need to score higher on standardized tests in order to gain admission into our country's most selective colleges. In reality, any test score gap between Asian

Americans and other students is not related to affirmative action because the same test score gaps exist whether a university considers race in its admissions policy or not." The test scores can be increased significantly by participation in expensive test-preparation courses. The scores are therefore socio-economically skewed in favor of students from wealthier families, who can afford to pay for test preparation courses.

In California, when a measure banned the consideration of race in university admissions, there was a plunge in underrepresented minority enrollments, the Asian advocacy group points out. The drop though was not offset by nonracial programs to increase diversity such as enrollments based on income, as the opponents of college quotas for minorities said it would. States that have attempted to use nonracial proxies, such as socioeconomic status, in order to increase racial diversity at schools and colleges have found that such proxies fail to wholly eliminate the barriers faced by many minorities.

Battle among Asian Tigers for College Admissions

One big hurdle Asian Americans face in getting admitted to the top American colleges is sharply rising competition from fellow Asians. From 2000 to 2015, the Asian population in America rose by 72%, reaching over 20 million, according to a Pew Research Center report. About a quarter of the Asians are Chinese and a fifth are Indians. The new immigrants settle in big metropolitan areas with large Asian populations like New York, Silicon Valley, Boston, Los Angeles, Washington D.C., Seattle, Philadelphia and Chicago.

Since they value good education, Asian parents push their children to study, get high test scores and get admitted to the top public schools. Wealthy Asians send their children to private schools. Asians hire tutors and spend much time and money on training their children to take part in math, science, music and other competitions, hoping to boost their chances of admission to a good college. Such aggressive Asians see themselves as tiger parents, a term widely used to describe them by the media.

In the major metropolitan regions, Asians compete for college admissions among themselves as well as with a very large number of qualified, non-Asian applicants, many of whose parents are educated, ambitious professionals. The top colleges admit a sizeable number of their students from these regions. But, over the past several decades, they have barely increased their capacity. So the number of students admitted from the big cities, as well as other parts of America and from abroad, have stayed roughly the same. Each year, due to the rapid rise in the Asian population and little or no increase in the total admissions, more Asian parents are disappointed that their children did not get in to a top college. Looking for easy answers, some Asian parents put the blame on the colleges for admitting Blacks and Hispanics.

Meanwhile the competition among Asians is getting tougher in the big cities due to electoral politics. In 2018, Blacks and Hispanics made up 67% of New York's public school population. But they together accounted for only 12% of the admissions to the top eight public high schools that year. A vast majority of the city's public school students, who are admitted to the top American colleges, are from these eight schools. The schools are free, like the rest of the public schools. So there is intense competition for admission to the top high schools. Asians have done well since selection was based purely on the results of a competitive entrance exam. In 2018, for instance, 52% of the students admitted were Asians; they are only 16% of New York city's population.

The city administration does not have the funds to invest in hiring and training good teachers and providing resources to raise the quality of all the public schools. Also, the politicians have little interest in such long-term solutions since they only care about winning the next elections. Instead, over a three year period starting in 2019, the Democratic mayor of New York plans to admit the top 7% of students from all middle schools to the top high schools, instead of using the three hour competitive entrance exam results. He is also similarly changing admission standards at some of the good public middle schools. Black and Hispanic leaders have welcomed the decisions as has *The New York Times*.

Asian American groups are protesting since the changes will reduce the number of Asians admitted to the top high schools. Such cuts in turn will likely result in fewer Asians from New York public schools getting admitted to the top American colleges. Asians have little political clout since they are few in numbers and are not major, well organized political donors.

White Conservatives Oppose Asian Admissions

While some Asian American groups are currently critical of the admission criteria for Blacks and Hispanics at the top colleges, their earlier complaints were about the admission of Whites. In the 1980's and 1990's, Asian groups lodged several complaints against the top colleges for denying admissions to highly qualified Asians while admitting Whites with lesser test scores. In 1986, as a result of one such complaint, an internal investigation by Stanford University found that "subconscious bias (towards Whites) by admissions officers was likely the culprit" for the wide differences in admission rates between equally qualified Whites and Asian American applicants.

In part due to public pressure, the top colleges began admitting more Asian Americans. From 1980 to 2015, their share of admissions rose sharply at all eight Ivy League colleges, according to a study by *The New York Times*. Meanwhile the admission of Whites declined to about 50% of the student population. At Caltech, for instance, the number of Asian

Americans exceeded Whites in 2015. Their numbers were roughly the same that year at the Massachusetts Institute of Technology.

The Asian American complaint and the lawsuits may lead to a few more seats for Asians at some of the top colleges. But it will also likely lead White conservative groups to target them next. Some White conservatives are already seeking cuts in the number of Asian American college admissions, to halt further declines in the admissions of Whites. "Engineering schools are all full of people from South Asia, and East Asia," Steve Bannon said in a media interview during the 2016 presidential election campaign. Bannon was Donald Trump's chief election strategist. He added that (White) American students "...can't get engineering degrees; they can't get into these graduate schools...When they come out, (the American students)...can't get a job."

The more logical target for middle-class Whites, as well as Asians, should be what Daniel Golden calls "the preferences of privilege" at the top colleges. As Golden points out in *ProPublica*, his 2006 book, *The Price of Admission*, discusses the preferences which "elevate predominantly white, affluent applicants: children of alumni, big non-alumni donors, politicians and celebrities, as well as recruited athletes in upper-crust sports like golf, sailing, horseback riding, crew and even, at some colleges, polo." The number of Whites who get privileged admissions outweigh the number of minorities aided by affirmative action, Golden notes. The preferences, he adds, "...displace more deserving candidates from other backgrounds, including Asian Americans and middle-class whites, without achieving the goals of affirmative action, such as diversity and redressing historical discrimination."

A Minority due to Geography, not Disadvantage

While some Indian Americans are loudly campaigning for college admissions to be based on merit, and in the process opposing other minorities, some are quietly seeking jobs and business opportunities reserved for minorities. Over the past three decades, courts as well as Republican and Democratic administrations have expanded efforts to end long-entrenched discrimination against women, Blacks, Hispanics, American Indians and other minorities. Such efforts are officially called affirmative actions.

In addition to college admissions, jobs and business contracts have been set aside for women and minorities by federal and state government agencies, train and road transport services, airport and port operators, numerous private companies, especially in government regulated businesses like phone, gas and electric utilities, banks, financial services, construction and educational institutions. The total annual value of business contracts reserved for women and minority owned small companies is quite large, well over $100 billion. In 2018, for instance, New York City's administration widely publicized that it set aside $17 billion for goods and services to be supplied by minority contractors.

There are some Indian Americans who get their business certified as minority owned in order to bid for contracts reserved for minorities. Some Indian women set up firms certified as double minorities, as being both women and Asian owned, to improve their chances of winning contracts. However the only reason Indians qualify as a minority is due to their being from Asia. They will fail a social and economic audit, if one were held, to determine their minority status. Indian American minority business owners don't meet the federal government's definition of being "small disadvantaged businesses...owned and controlled by socially and economically disadvantaged individuals."

Up until the 1970's, "whole industries and categories of employment were, in effect, all-white, all-male. In thousands of towns and cities, police departments and fire departments remained all white and male; Women and minorities were forbidden to even apply," notes a White House document, prepared during Bill Clinton's Presidency, 1992 to 2000. Indians who claim minority status have emigrated to America since the 1970's, in pursuit of high-paying professional careers. They are from middle and upper class families in India and mostly educated at the top Indian and American universities.

There is little or no media coverage of Indians who run minority owned businesses. This is in sharp contrast to the wide attention paid to the success of Indians in other fields in America. The Indian minority businesses avoid publicity, fearing that scrutiny will reveal that they compete unfairly against Blacks, Hispanics and other minorities. It is likely that White conservative groups, emboldened by President Trump's policies, will lobby and legally challenge the job and business quotas set aside for minorities, especially Asians. If this happens, Indians who have minority status will find it tough to justify their claims. Their educational qualifications and socio-economic background will clearly show that they don't deserve any government help.

Chapter 5

CANADA AND CHINA BENEFIT FROM U.S. VISA POLICIES

In the 2016 U.S. presidential election, over 70 percent of Indian-Americans voted for Hilary Clinton, according to several surveys. Though mostly Hindu, they were not persuaded by the Republican Hindu Coalition to back Donald Trump. Indians in America are troubled by the rise in racism since Trump began his election campaign.

Ravin Gandhi, for instance, was a big supporter of Hilary Clinton. Initially he expected good business policies from President Trump and decided to back him. But in August 2017, after a White racist rally in Virginia, he "...saw the president of the United States cowardly signal tacit support of white supremacists and Nazis...I will not in good conscience support a president who seems to hate Americans who don't look like him," Gandhi wrote on the website of *CNBC*, the business news television channel.

Following publication of his comments, Gandhi's office email and voicemail were swamped with attacks from Trump supporters. "You are angry for having been born with 50 percent negro blood in your veins," one of them wrote. Gandhi told the *The Chicago Tribune* that "...the sad reality is there's a group of racists in the USA that views me as a second-class citizen...people thought my professional position somewhat protected me." He added the nasty emailers and callers are a fringe element of Trump supporters. But as president, Gandhi said, Trump sets the tone and "…his moral leadership on this issue is reprehensible."

Based in Chicago, Gandhi is co-founder of GMM Nonstick Coatings, a global supplier of coatings for cookware and bakeware. GMM, with 240 employees, was sold to a Japanese company in 2016. A son of Indian immigrants, Gandhi has a B.S. from the University of Illinois, an MBA from Northwestern University and is a Certified Public Accountant. He also runs Glenborn Partners, an investment fund he founded in 2002.

Canada is Open for Business

While racism continues to rise, the opportunities for professionals from India to emigrate to America are shrinking. Universities are eliminating or slashing financial aid to foreign students due to smaller budgets. Trump's policies of cutting skilled worker, student training and spousal visas will likely be in place for a long time. Even if the next President is a liberal, free trade Democrat, he or she may be unable to reverse Trump's policies. The visa cuts are supported by professional organizations of engineers and other IT employees, labor unions and several Democratic lawmakers.

More important, many technology and other companies in America are tackling the shrinking supply of skilled foreign labor, in order to grow and protect their profit margins. Without attracting publicity, they are pursuing greater automation at their U.S. operations. They are also setting up and expanding operations abroad; technology companies notably in Canada. Once such major changes to cut costs are initiated by a management, they have a momentum of their own and are unlikely to be reversed.

The Canadian government is making a strong pitch to

attract top foreign talent, especially after Trump's election. Its slogan: "Canada is open for business." Canada faces a shortage of skilled labor and also has a population which is rapidly aging. "Five million Canadians are set to retire by 2035...We are emphatically and unapologetically taking the opposite approach (to America.) We welcome the innovation...the entrepreneurial spirits, and the unique skill sets of skilled newcomers," Ahmed Hussen, Canada's immigration minister said in 2017. The country, with a population of 36 million, has a low unemployment rate of around 5%. It has introduced several measures to attract skilled foreigners: making it easier to get student visas; granting visas for advanced skilled workers within two weeks of application and others within six months; offering visas to entrepreneurs; and providing over $50 million for skills training of new immigrants. By 2020, the government's goal is to admit one million immigrants a year, "the most ambitious immigration levels in recent Canadian history," the minister said.

A Push for Artificial Intelligence Research

The Canadian government wants the country to be a leader in Artificial Intelligence (AI) and machine learning research and businesses. It set up and helped fund the Vector Institute at the University of Toronto, an AI teaching and research center. The institute has attracted $150 million in funding, including from Google, Uber Technologies and Nvidia, an American computer chip maker, as well as from major Canadian companies. Its goal is to attract the "best global talent...to drive the application, adoption and commercialization" of AI across Canada.

The Vector Institute is located in a technology hub, the MaRS Discovery District, across from the University of Toronto. About 150 medical, AI and other startups as well as IBM, Autodesk and Merck have offices in the district. By 2022, the Vector Institute plans to graduate 1,000 Master's students each year. Geoffrey Hinton, the chief advisor to the institute, is one of three pioneers in AI and machine learning. He works for Google in Toronto. Another pioneer is Yoshua Bengio, who heads the Montreal Institute of Learning Algorithms (MILA.) It's a public private institute conducting research in machine learning and neural network systems. About 50 Ph.D. and Master's students are affiliated with it through programs run by McGill, Montreal and two other universities in Quebec. Waterloo, Queens and other top Canadian universities are also expanding their offerings of computer science and advanced technology programs.

Bengio, a professor at the University of Montreal, co-founded Element AI. It helps large companies use AI to solve major business problems. Element has 70 Ph.D.s from 15 countries among its staff of 270. It wants to add more researchers but is unable to find them. There are few graduates who have the combination of skills in mathematics, statistics, data analysis and computer coding, which is required for AI jobs. Also, there is big demand for such graduates, with some stars being paid over a million dollars a year by Google, Facebook, Uber, Nvidia and other big American companies.

Companies pursuing AI and other new technologies in Canada are unlikely to employ hundreds of thousands of engineers and math and science graduates. But their success, and more so Trump's visa policies, are attracting start-ups as well as large companies and creating jobs in Canada. Major players in the technology food chain in America, of start-ups, managers and venture funds, are moving to Canada. In 2017, for instance, the co-founders of Palantir, Addepar, Zenreach and other major American technological companies, set up Terminal. With offices in suburban Toronto, Montreal and Vancouver, it provides technical talent to Eventbrite, Plays.tv and other American emerging companies. Terminal is backed by Sequoia Capital,

Khosla Ventures and other top American venture funds. Dylan Serota, a co-founder told the *Financial Times*, "It is now the tech-elites versus the Trump Administration, and it is very difficult to find common ground for economic growth (in America.) A lot of other countries are very tech-forward, building partnerships with tech companies."

Evading Trump's Visa Policies
by Setting up in Canada

Major American companies are setting up and expanding their operations in Canada, apparently to bypass the restrictions on hiring skilled foreigners that they face in the U.S. Apple, Amazon, Microsoft and IBM have expanded their offices in Canada, while Uber has opened new offices. In 2017, Google and Facebook opened offices in Edmonton and Montreal to find the best global AI talent. Sara Sabour is an Iranian who ended up in Toronto, after she was denied a visa to study in the United States, according to *The New York Times*. She is an AI expert working for Google under Geoffrey Hinton.

In October 2017, a subsidiary of Google's parent Alphabet announced it is investing $50 million to develop 3.3 million square feet of commercial, retail and residential space. The buildings, including a new headquarters for Google Canada, will be built on 12 acres in Toronto's old port area. If the project succeeds, the government plans to invite Alphabet to help develop another 750 acres in the area.

The flow of talented emigrants to Canada will have an adverse, long-term impact on U.S. high technology and other businesses and jobs. When an employee joins a start-up in Toronto, instead of one in New York, the "wider impact will be felt, literally, for decades," Kevin Ryan told *The New York Times*. Some of the employees will launch their own start-ups, further strengthening the attraction of Toronto to foreign students and new businesses. Zola, a web-based wedding gift registry Ryan founded, is among the American companies hiring staff in Canada through Terminal.

Ryan is a serial entrepreneur who founded several successful companies in America: Doubleclick, an online advertising platform, bought by Google for $3.1 billion in 2007; *Business Insider*, a web-based business publication, bought by Axel Springer, Germany's leading digital publisher, for $450 million in 2015; Gilt Group, a web-based luxury goods retailer; MongoDB, a database platform run by Dev Ittycheria, an Indian engineer. Several former employees of Ryan's companies have gone on to found their own companies. A graduate of Yale and an MBA from INSEAD, Ryan is on the board or adviser to eleven companies. Ryan's philanthropic work includes serving on the board of Human Rights Watch, board of the Yale Corporation and as chair of the Partnership for New York City's Innovation Council.

More Indians move to Canada

There are very few Indians working for AI and other new technology companies in Canada. Till recently, graduates of the Indian Institutes of Technology and India's top math and science colleges were not interested in pursuing advanced degrees at universities in Canada. But this is changing due to the rising prestige of the AI institutes in Toronto, Montreal and elsewhere, the high salaries their graduates command, the ease of getting Canadian work visas that will help them repay their education loans and English being the language of business. The other major attraction for Indian professionals is the prospect of being hired by one of the American companies expanding in Canada, since such jobs may pay more and offer merit-based career prospects.

In 2016, about 18,000 Indians were admitted to Canadian

colleges and universities. Indians also got about 39,000 of the 300,000 work visas issued to foreigners by Canada that year. Two thirds of the visas were given to skilled workers, with the rest going to family members and refugees. Since Trump's election, the number of Indians applying to Canadian colleges has risen sharply. In 2017, for instance, the University of Toronto saw a 59% jump in applications from Indians. Big companies as well as start-ups in Canada are seeing a sharp increase in applicants from fresh graduates and employees from America. These are foreigners, many of them Indians, who cannot get work and permanent residency visas in the U.S. "I've been in tech for over 20 years in Canada and in Silicon Valley, too. I've never seen candidates from the U.S. apply for Canadian positions from places like Silicon Valley," Roy Pereira, the CEO of Zoom.ai, told *Axios*. Zoom is a Toronto based company that provides automated assistants that perform tasks like scheduling meetings, introducing people and organizing travel.

Vikram Rangnekar set up MovNorth.com, a blog to guide Indians and other foreigners in America to find jobs and get permanent resident visas in Canada. He worked as a software engineer at LinkedIn in the Silicon Valley for six years. He did not want the uncertainty and additional ten years of waiting to get a permanent residency status in America. In 2017, Rangnekar decided to emigrate to Canada with his wife and children. A few months after his application, he got a Canadian permanent residency visa. In Toronto, he founded Webmatr, a platform which helps developers create mobile apps. He is also a partner at Global Skills Hub, that is helping Canadian companies find skilled foreigners. After finishing high school in Mumbai, he got a B.S. in computer science from the University of Delaware in the U.S.

Rangnekar says on his blog that the whole point of the move from America to Canada "was to get more freedom and some peace of mind" with a permanent resident visa. Also he must be happy to have stopped paying social security taxes in America. The annual taxes are 6.2% for employees and 12.4% for business owners, up to $128,400 in income. Rangnekar cannot claim social security payments from the American government when he retires at 65, even though he paid the taxes for six years.

In February 2018, Prime Minister Justin Trudeau led a large Canadian delegation to India, which included five of his ministers. While they spent a week in the country, their visit was not a diplomatic success. Both the Indian and Canadian media described it as one of Trudeau's failures. Senior Indian officials ignored the delegation over the Canadian government's support of Sikh groups in Canada. (See Appendix D for the background to this issue.) But evidently the focus of the visit not diplomacy but attracting India's top talent to Canada. The delegation toured major Indian cities to promote the message to students and professionals that it has become easier to get advanced degrees and jobs in Canada.

Will Indians Boost Chinese Companies?

Besides businesses in Canada, Chinese companies will likely start hiring more of India's engineers and math graduates. The companies are technology leaders in several fields from solar panels to web-based retailing and e-payments. "In one generation many segments of China's technology industry have achieved what took a century in Silicon Valley," notes Michael Moritz in his blog. China has four silicon valleys while America has just one. Chinese entrepreneurs combine innovation, opportunism and intuition just like the bold names of the Western technology universe, Moritz continues. He is a venture investor at Sequoia Capital, based in Menlo Park, California. The companies Sequoia funded have a total public market value of $3.3 trillion.

By 2025, the Chinese government wants China to also be the global leader in AI, robotics, electric and autonomous vehicles, drones, 3-D printing and other new technologies. Major Chinese companies are expanding their research and development facilities outside China as their business expands globally. Some of them are competing with American companies to hire the best global talent from Stanford, Massachusetts Institute of Technology and other top universities. They will likely start hiring India's top engineering and math graduates for their operations in Canada, Europe and Southeast Asia.

In America, Padmasree Warrior is a notable Indian hire by a Chinese company. In 2015, she was appointed chief development officer and U.S. chief executive of Nio. She leads a team of over 300 engineers and other employees based in California. The company is testing a fleet of autonomous electric vehicles. It is creating a comfortable "living space" for passengers traveling in the car, Warrior told *Business Insider*. Since the car drives itself, she added, a passenger can sleep, watch movies, and take conference calls.

Nio will introduce its first vehicle in China in 2018 and in the U.S. in 2020. It is estimated to be priced below $100,000, competing against Tesla's high-end vehicles. Nio has raised over $1 billion from Chinese giants Tencent and Baidu as well as America's Sequoia Capital. Warrior, who is on the board of directors at Microsoft, was earlier chief technology officer at Cisco Systems. She has an M.S. from Cornell University and a B.S. from IIT Delhi, both in chemical engineering.

There is friction between India and China. They fought a war in 1962. Only a third of Indians view China favorably, while only a quarter of Chinese have a good opinion of India, according to a 2016 Pew Research Center study. India has a big trade deficit with China. In fiscal year 2017, India imported $62 billion of products from China, including consumer goods and electrical and manufacturing machinery and parts. India's exports to China totaled only $10 billion that year, mainly commodities like ores and cotton. In 2018, the Indian government increased tariffs on imports of Chinese toys, watches, furniture, footwear, beauty aids as well as solar panels, mobile phones, TVs and parts related to these products.

Yet diplomatic and business ties continue to grow between India and China. India sees China as a source of much-needed capital to grow its economy as well as a counter weight to America. China wants India to stay neutral in its geo-political contest with America. Also, Chinese companies are eager to sell more goods and services to India. Meanwhile more Indians are learning Chinese since there is rising demand for staff from the Chinese companies operating in India. Several private tutoring schools teach Chinese in major Indian cities, with some of them offering courses in conjunction with high schools.

Chinese companies are also major investors in several Indian start-ups which face strong competition from American companies. For instance, China's Alibaba and one of its subsidiaries have invested $880 million in Paytm and its retail arm. Paytm is India's leading digital payments company. The demand for mobile payments is growing very rapidly, with the spread of smartphone use. The market is estimated to reach $500 billion in annual transactions in 2020, up from just $50 billion in 2016. Paytm's founder Vijay Shankar Sharma told *Knowledge@Wharton that* the company plans to invest $760 million to upgrade its technology, from 2018 to 2020. The company has already invested a similar amount.

Sharma graduated from high school at 14 and from the Delhi College of Engineering at the age of 19. Initially he was handicapped by his lack of proficiency in English. In college, since he could not follow the classes in English, he used both Hindi and English textbooks. He taught himself to code and designed a content management software, which was used by *The Indian Express* and other publishers. After graduating, he funded his start-up by taking on a $14,000 loan, for which he paid 24% in annual interest. In 2017, Paytm raised $1.4 billion from Softbank. The payments company is valued at about $10 billion. This implies that Sharma, the 39-year-old son of a school teacher from the small town of Aligarh, has an estimated net worth of $1.7 billion.

Sharma's goal is to build India's first company with $100 billion in annual revenues, which he says would be a source of pride for the country. As he continues his quest, he has repeatedly complained to the Indian government about unfair competition from Facebook, Amazon and Google. He says the American companies ignore regulations in India. Explaining why he chose to partner with a Chinese company, Sharma told the *Economic Times,* "I never had the money to go to Stanford or MIT...I researched a lot on e-commerce" businesses before teaming up with Jack Ma and his Alibaba.

Chapter 6

LESS DEMAND FOR
INDIA'S TOP ENGINEERS

In 2017, the impact of the shifts in technology and Trump's policies led to over 200,000 employees losing their jobs at IT companies in India. They included about 60,000 engineers. The job losses are more than three times the typical annual turnover of IT employees in India. Management jobs were also cut, something that has rarely happened. While senior executives at the companies are silent, Indian government officials deny that jobs are being cut. Those losing jobs are "non-performers" with "irrelevant skills" and they must gain new skills, an official from the Indian IT Ministry told the media.

Meanwhile the fired employees have a tough time dealing with the first major industry-wide job cuts they face. "I have an 11-year-old child. My wife is not working. How to pay the home loans?" a 41-year-old engineer in Pune, who lost his job, told Nida Najar of *The New York Times*. After being with the Indian IT company for 11 years, he was let go with two months' pay and a bonus totaling $3,200. He has 10 more years of payments left on a loan he took to buy an apartment and got just one unsuccessful job interview. Some of those losing jobs are hiding the news from their families. Others are going to astrologers to find solutions. Some, in their desperation to find a job, are being swindled into paying thousands of dollars to recruiters promising to find them high-paying jobs.

Unemployed Computer Engineers

Many fresh engineering graduates are also not finding jobs. In 2017, for instance, a third of the 9,100 graduates of the Indian Institutes of Technology (IIT) had no job offers, according to *The Hindustan Times*. This is in part because there were more graduates seeking jobs in India. Very few of them left to study for advanced degrees at American universities or found jobs outside India. Also, there is limited demand for them from IT companies in India. The domestic market for IT services is relatively small, with major Indian IT companies getting only a quarter of their revenues from clients in India. They are also facing rising costs and slowing demand in the U.S., their major foreign market.

In addition, there is a mismatch in talent. Almost all IIT students, not just those in computer and electrical engineering programs, spend most of their time learning IT and related skills on their own. They do this expecting to find lucrative IT jobs, preferably in America, upon graduation. When there was a drop in hiring for IT jobs in 2017, many mechanical, industrial and civil engineering IIT graduates could not find jobs in their industries. They do not have the skills and career interest. Also the non-IT companies, as well as some IT companies, are reluctant to hire them, fearing they will leave when they find a better paying job.

The inability of IIT graduates to find jobs is a major setback for the future of higher education in India. By 2022, Prime Minister Narendra Modi wants to attract over $18 billion from private investors to boost digital businesses, including by connecting every village to the internet. Implementing this plan requires a big increase in the number of computer science and other high technology graduates. But Modi's government has very limited funds to set up new schools and colleges, expand and improve existing facilities as well as subsidize the fees. So he is trying to get private investors to build the educational institutions.

India has a vast pool of students who can learn computer, internet, math and other advanced technology skills. But their parents, being poor or middle-class, do not earn enough to pay the high fees charged by private colleges. Modi expects parents will take on educational loans, eager to help their children find better careers. But most private professional colleges have a bad reputation since their graduates do not find jobs that pay enough to help repay their education loans.

India's World Class Engineers and Doctors

Indians have a high respect for education and are eager to learn and find good jobs. Education is extremely cheap due to government subsidies. Yet most Indians do not finish high school since they are forced to take up jobs to support their families. Only 5% of Indians have college degrees, while an additional 1% have post-high school technical training. The world renowned engineers, scientists and doctors, which India produces each year, are a tiny fraction of the country's student population. They are mostly from English language-based schools and colleges. They pass a series of fiercely competitive exams to emerge as graduates of the best and most selective professional colleges.

The top engineering, medical, management, science, dental, pharmacy and nursing colleges in India are run by the government. It also provides the funding, including heavily subsidizing the total costs for a degree. In 2017 for instance, the annual fees and other costs at the Indian Institute of Technology (IIT) Madras totaled about $4,000. This was for a student from a family whose parents are in the top income bracket. The total costs for students from low-income families was under $2,000 a year. This is less than 10% of the costs of attending the top privately run engineering colleges in India.

Competition for admission to the best government-run professional colleges is intense, given the low fees, high reputation and prospects for finding well-paying jobs. In 2016, 10,500 engineering students - less than 1% of applicants - were admitted to the 23 campuses of the world-renowned IITs. The chances of admission are equally low for applicants for the 2,000 seats at the seven All India Institute of Medical Sciences (AIIMS) as well as at the other top medical colleges. In addition, each year second tier colleges admit an additional 50,000 engineering students and an equal number of medical students, selecting about 5% of applicants. In management, there are about 30 reputed MBA programs, including at the 19 Indian Institutes of Management (IIM). In 2016, about 4,000 students, or 2% of applicants, were selected to the IIMs. Some of the colleges, especially the second-tier engineering and medical colleges, do not have good teachers. But the students are motivated, high achievers with strong work habits, who learn much on their own and from each other.

Admission to the top and second-tier government-run colleges is based on entrance exams in physics, chemistry and either mathematics, for applicants to engineering colleges, or biology for medical college applicants. Affluent parents send their children to private for-profit tutoring schools to prepare for the entrance exams. The best tutoring schools hold their own entrance exams for selecting students. The fees at the tutoring schools are several multiples of the annual fees charged by the government-run professional colleges.

Government-run colleges reserve seats for low-caste, backward-caste, tribal, regional and other applicants. The scores on the entrance exams, required for admission to the reserved quotas, are lower than those gotten by applicants admitted from the general pool. The exam scores of all accepted applicants, as well as the number of reserved seats, is publicly disclosed by the colleges. Reservation of seats is a major issue in Indian politics. (This issues is discussed in Appendix C.)

The government has also funded a National Program for Technology Enhanced Learning, set up jointly by five IITs and the Institute of Science, Bangalore. It provides over 200 video and web based courses on engineering and science topics, covered over four to twelve weeks. While the courses are free, there is a $30 fee for those interested in taking a certifying exam. The goal is to train teachers, mid-career professionals and students interested in pursuing advanced degrees.

Microsoft CEO Satya Nadella failed the IIT exam

There are several professional colleges run by religious, philanthropic and business groups. Private colleges, which do not reserve seats based on government quotas, get little or no government funds. Admission is based on the ability to pay the total costs and, at the good private colleges, on results of competitive entrance exams. They charge an admission fee, which is as high as $75,000 at some colleges. The annual tuition and other fees total around $15,000 at some of the reputed engineering and management colleges. The students who study at these colleges are those who did not get admitted to the government-run colleges. They are mostly from wealthy families. Some middle-class parents borrow loans from banks to pay the high fees.

A few private colleges are high-quality institutions, including the two Christian Medical Colleges and Manipal University. Satya Nadella, the chief executive of Microsoft, got a degree in electronics engineering from Manipal in 1988. He had failed the IIT entrance exam. After Manipal he got a Master's in electrical engineering from the University of Wisconsin,

86

Milwaukee. Later, while working at Microsoft, he got an MBA from the University of Chicago. Rajiv Suri, chief executive of Nokia, also graduated as an electronics engineer from Manipal.

Some of the private colleges reserve seats based on religious and other criteria. For instance, Manipal reserves 15% of seats for students of Indian origin, living outside India. The total costs for such students is comparable to those at private colleges in the U.S. In 2017, Manipal charged them $208,000 for its four-and-a-half year medical degree.

Most of the private colleges provide an inferior education and charge very high fees, especially in the case of popular job-oriented programs. They burden middle-class students and parents with loans which many cannot repay. For instance, private institutions run over 2,500 MBA and over 2,000 engineering colleges, since there is great demand for such degrees. But graduates of only about the top 50 of such for-profit colleges find jobs with wages high enough to help them repay their educational loans within ten years.

Golden Age for Indian Students in America

From the 1970's to about 2016, graduates of the top engineering, medical and science schools found it more attractive, financially and career-wise, to pursue advanced degrees in America than take up a job in India. American universities eagerly admitted Indian students to their Master's and Ph.D. programs. Such graduate students tutored, graded and did much of the course preparation and teaching of under-graduate courses. They also helped the faculty with their research and writing and did administrative tasks. It was far cheaper for American Universities to give assistantships and fellowships to Indian students, that covered their fees and all other expenses, than to hire full-time, permanent staff to do the work. Also, Americans with engineering, medical and science under-graduate degrees were finding good jobs and so very few of them were interested in studying for advanced degrees.

The quality of the top Indian students is very high. Vinod Khosla, a billionaire venture capitalist in Silicon Valley, told *CBS TV* that when he was at Carnegie Mellon for a Master's degree in 1978, "I thought I was cruising all the way because it was so easy relative to the education I had got at IIT (Delhi.)" Like Khosla, hundreds of thousands of Indian students got teaching assistantships and fellowships to study for advanced degrees at U.S. universities. Many of them abandoned their Ph.D. programs, after they got a Master's degree, to take up high-paying jobs in America. They were hired on work visas by the fast-growing computer and information technology companies and other high technology businesses. The American universities did not object since each year they got a fresh batch of graduate students from India. Also, the hiring of their Master's graduates enhanced their reputation among future applicants.

American Universities Cut Financial Aid

Since the 2008-2009 recession, American universities have sharply reduced the number and value of financial grants offered to graduate students. This is because most of them, especially the state-run and smaller private universities, face repeated budget cuts. Also, the federal and state governments are giving them less funding for research and other projects. Meanwhile the costs have risen rapidly due to faculty and staff hires and construction of new buildings and other facilities.

American universities are seeking to raise revenues by enrolling more students for Master's degrees as well as offering several new programs. New York University, for instance, offers over a hundred Master's degrees and certifications. Its business school offers over a dozen more programs, in addition to an MBA. The programs offered are nine months to two years in length, with many universities offering both part-time and full-time options. The specializations range from data science, financial engineering and risk management to museum studies, performance studies and art therapy. The main criteria for admission, to the esoteric programs at the major universities and for most programs at the lower quality universities, is the ability to pay the full costs. Up until Trump's attacks on immigrants and his visa restrictions, there was big demand, especially at universities in New York, Boston, San Francisco and other major cities. Hundreds of thousands of foreigners from wealthy families enjoyed a few years in America on a student visa.

Most Indians are interested in pursuing job-oriented Master's degrees in America. Universities do not offer financial aid that covers the total costs because they do not have the funds and since there is big demand for the programs from foreign students. For instance, during the 2015-16 academic year, foreigners accounted for nearly 80% of the 2,868 students in the Master's programs at New York University's Tandon School of Engineering. The school's fees and costs total over $90,000 a year.

For the Master's programs, instead of sizeable financial aid, universities offer scholarships to several students. But these are viewed as marketing teasers by students since they cover only about 10% of the total costs. Some Indian students feel honored to be awarded a scholarship, especially by the major universities. If they are not from wealthy families, they take on large educational loans to pay for the remaining 90% of the fees and costs. Students pursuing degrees in science, technology, engineering and math assume they have a safety option. They could find jobs in America for up to 29 months under practical training visas. Such jobs, they reason, will enable them to repay a big part of their educational loans, even if they have to return to India.

Risk of Losing Family Homes to Study in the U.S.

Indian students in America face rising competition for practical training and skilled-worker visas from other foreigners, especially the Chinese and South Koreans. Since 2014, the demand for skilled worker visas has far exceeded 85,000, which is the maximum number issued each year. More important, since Donald Trump became President in 2017, his administration has effectively cut the number of practical training and skilled worker visas issued. In 2017, for instance, only six of 41 applicants got skilled worker visas in a New York city program to create jobs by sponsoring foreign entrepreneurs. Trump's administration plans to soon eliminate this visa as well as reduce the number and length of practical training visas granted to foreign students. It is also going to stop issuing work visas for spouses of skilled worker visa holders. These measures will hurt Indians pursuing advanced degrees in America, including those studying engineering, math, technology and science.

The prospects are far worse for thousands of Indians studying business, economics, international affairs and other social science courses at American universities. Far fewer of them get any financial aid from the universities and so their educational loans are larger. Their practical training visa lasts for only a year, assuming they can find a job. So unless their families are wealthy enough to pay the full costs, even an MBA from a top school takes on a big financial burden. In 2018, for instance, a student enrolled for the two year MBA at Columbia University in New York will incur about $216,000 in total costs, including $144,000 for tuition fees. The median annual salary offered to 2017 Columbia MBA graduates was $146,000. So assuming students from India get an American work visa and a job which pays them around the median salary – both very big assumptions - it will take them at least ten years to repay their education loans.

In 2017, six percent or more of the MBAs from Columbia, Northwestern, New York, Virginia, Vanderbilt, Indiana and Emory universities had no job offers three months after their graduation. Most of them were likely Indians and other foreign students. Indians returning to India, with American MBAs, will take 20 years or more to repay the loans. The financial burden is worse for Indians who take on bank loans to pursue advanced social science degrees in America. They face a very high risk of defaulting on their loans and losing their family homes to the banks.

Low-Risk Strategy of IIT Graduates

Indians considering Master's degrees in management and social sciences in America, and who do not have the money, should do two things. They should avoid taking on education loans if they cannot repay it back within ten years, while working at a job in India. Second, following the example of many IIT graduates, they should follow a low-risk strategy. In recent years, IIT graduates continue to be admitted to American universities. But few of them enroll since they do not get financial aid that covers most of their total costs. In 2016, for instance, less than 15% of graduating IIT students went to the U.S. for advanced degrees, compared to 80% during the 1990's. Also that year, only 200 - or 2% of the graduates – found jobs outside India. America was not the top source of jobs. At IIT Bombay, for instance, thirty five graduates went to Japan while only ten were hired to work in America.

IIT officials say that most graduates stayed in India because they got high-paying jobs at the local offices of Google, Apple, Facebook, Microsoft and other major American and foreign technology and business companies. But IIT students know that fewer Indians are finding practical training and permanent jobs in the U.S., after their American degrees. They also see that those returning to India from America have a tough time repaying their educational loans. So most IIT graduates do not want to borrow $100,000 to $200,000 from banks, by putting up their family home as collateral, in order to study in America. Instead they pursue the safer route of taking up jobs at Microsoft, Uber, Google, Apple and other major foreign companies in India. The starting pay is about $30,000 a year, a third of what they would be paid if they can get a visa and job in America. But it is the top wage level in India, which provides a very good lifestyle. The engineers plan to work for the foreign companies in India for a few years and then try to get the company to transfer them to a much higher paying assignment in a foreign country.

Chapter 7

END OF GROWTH FOR
INDIAN IT COMPANIES?

India's top engineers have created a large information technology (IT) services business in the country. Two thirds of the global IT services work, which is sent offshore, is performed in India. Since inception about forty years ago, total revenues have grown rapidly reaching over $150 billion in 2017. The business accounts for about 10% of India's Gross Domestic Product. It directly and indirectly provides jobs for over 20 million in Bangalore, Hyderabad, Gurgaon, Mumbai, Pune and other cities. The indirect jobs, which are estimated to be over four times the number of IT employees, include workers at the office complexes, residential towers, restaurants, bars, health clubs and other businesses as well as helpers who provide cooking, cleaning and other services at the homes of the IT employees.

The 1990's IT Boom & Bust Creates Billionaires in India

During the 1980's, the operations of American financial and service companies were being increasingly computerized, especially following the spread of personal computers. At the same time, new high-speed telecommunication services provided more reliable, faster and cheaper connections between the U.S. and

India. American IT workers did not want to do tedious work like writing repetitive code for large software programs. The salaries were low, the work was boring and many of the offices were white-collar sweatshops. Such work was outsourced by American companies to Infosys, Wipro and other emerging companies in India. The work was done for a fraction of what it would cost in the U.S. since wages in India were roughly 25% of those paid to similar staff in America. There was a large supply of good quality engineers and math graduates in India who were eager to work in IT jobs since the pay was much higher than that at other jobs.

The American companies found the IT work done in India, by fluent English-language speakers, to be of good quality. Following the 1990 economic recession, American companies sought to cut costs and raise profits by moving more IT-based tasks to India. Several back office tasks were sent to India, including pay roll, record keeping as well as some development of software. In addition, the declining costs of computers and telecommunication systems led to thousands of less-skilled, lower-wage jobs, such as telephone call-based customer services, being moved from America to India.

Starting in the mid-1990s, there was a big surge in IT and back office work outsourced to India. Wages for engineers and other skilled IT staff in America were rising sharply due to demand from thousands of new internet companies. Also, in the U.S. and Europe there were widespread fears that older computer systems would crash and cripple operations when the date switched to the year 2000 - the Y2K problem. The work on the software patches, to "fix" the problem, could be done cheaply in India. Looking back it appears the Y2K fears may have been a marketing strategy of the IT companies and consultants to sell more hardware, software and consultancy services. On January 1, 2000, planes took off and landed safely at Russian airports even though computer systems were not upgraded to handle the Y2K threat.

Internet and most technology stocks were crushed in America, following the 2000-2002 collapse of the internet bubble. As a result, funding for most companies in these businesses was cut off, reducing their demand for IT staff. At the same time, facing an economic recession, American companies sought to cut costs by moving more jobs to India. In the early 2000's, about half a million jobs are estimated to have been eliminated in the U.S. and moved to India. They included jobs in accounting, filing income taxes, clinical drug research, debt collection, and equity and bond analysis. "Everything that you can send down a wire is up for grabs," Nandan Nilekani told the World Economic Forum in January 2004. Nilekani was then chief executive of Infosys Technologies, the second largest Indian IT firm. The booming IT outsourcing business in India created several billionaires, including Nilekani and the other founders of Infosys. Following the Great Recession of 2008-2009, triggered by the collapse of the U.S. housing bubble, many more jobs were outsourced to India.

Technology Changes Hurt Indian IT companies

In the early 2010's, IT companies in India were hit with surging wages and high annual turnover of skilled employees. This was in part due to rising demand for staff from the Indian operations of Microsoft, Google, IBM, Oracle and other American and other foreign companies. The American companies were seeking to sell more products and services in India as well as reduce costs by getting more of their work done in India. They are able to hire the best local talent since they offer better wages, benefits and employment terms than the Indian companies. The wages they pay in India though are less than a third of what they would pay for similarly qualified engineers in the U.S.

Indian IT companies were also hurt by the limited supply of high-quality engineering, math and science graduates in India. So, to counter rising wages, they began automating their operations. For instance, from 2010 to 2015, the revenues of Tata Consultancy Services grew by a compound annual 20% while its employee hiring grew by a slower 15%. The reduced pace of hiring was due to a rise in automation, notes a 2016 research report on Indian IT services companies by Centrum, an investment bank which is based in Mumbai.

At Wipro, automation enabled the company to "release" 4,300 jobs during the first three quarters of fiscal year 2016. By 2020, Infosys wants to raise profitability by lifting revenues per employee from around $50,000 a year to $80,000, according to Centrum. Infosys' 2017 annual report notes that, through the use of automation, it eliminated about "11,000 full-time employees worth of effort" and re-trained them to perform new tasks. The "re-training" affected more than 5% of its employees. The company had about 200,000 employees worldwide at the end of fiscal year 2017.

Hit by President Trump's Policies

Indian IT companies get about three quarters of their revenues from work done for foreign clients, mainly in the U.S. So they are also being hit by President Trump's anti-immigration policies. In fiscal year 2017, the top seven Indian IT companies received 9,356 new H-1 B skilled worker visas, a sharp drop of 37% from the previous year, according to a study by the National Foundation for American Policy. The lobbying group, which supports more visa issuance for skilled immigrants, expects the drop in visas for Indian IT companies to be even sharper in fiscal year 2018.

IT services companies typically bill clients based on the number of employees assigned to a task and the hours they work. So getting fewer work visas in 2017 meant that the top seven

Indian IT companies saw their revenues in the U.S. shrink at least by an estimated $600 million. Their profit margins in America must also have shrunk due to higher pay for Indians hired on skilled worker visas, as required by Trump's policies, the hiring of higher-cost American staff and the drop in revenues.

In May 2017, Infosys announced it will create 10,000 jobs in the U.S. It started hiring engineers and software developers in Indianapolis and forecasts hiring 2,000 people in the city by 2022. This will be the second largest job creation in the state of Indiana, since Honda hired 2,064 workers for its factory in 2007, according to *IndyStar*. Indiana is the home state of Mike Pence who is Trump's vice-president. The state is giving $31 million in tax concessions and other incentives to Infosys. The agreement was reached quickly, in under three months of negotiations. This indicates either an eager Indiana state administration or perhaps that Infosys was under pressure to quickly announce creation of American jobs, in order to be able to bid for some major contracts or avoid current contracts not being renewed.

Indian IT Companies Miss the Shift to New Technologies

The bigger, long term threat to Indian IT companies is disruption from recent technological changes. Many technology businesses are destroyed in a decade or two as customers shift to new products and services sold by emerging competitors. Indian IT companies were fortunate to prosper for nearly four decades. This was because they were users of technology and not manufacturers. Also, they serviced clients using new generations of computer hardware and software, which got more efficient and cheaper but changed very little.

Since the 2010s, the spread of smartphones, tablets and cheap, easy to download mobile applications enables American employees and consumers to access most services without help from the IT staff. The spread of these technologies has reduced the demand for services provided by Indian IT companies. Also, much of the IT infrastructure, support and back office functions have moved to cloud based systems which are dominated by giants like Amazon, Microsoft, Google and Oracle. This has slashed IT departments at U.S. based companies and evaporated the billion dollar outsourcing contracts enjoyed by Indian IT companies, points out Vivek Wadhwa in an opinion piece in *The Washington Post* in 2017.

In recent years, American companies have been rapidly expanding the use of automation, robotics, machine learning, big data analytics and other forms of artificial intelligence (AI,) cloud-based services, sensors, and cyber security. They see the new technologies helping them sell new products and services as well as increasing their efficiency, security and profits. The vendors of automation technologies in the U.S. are getting a boost from President Trump's work visa policies. Instead of paying more to hire Americans as Trump wants, several American companies are quietly pursuing more automation. Anticipating such rise in demand, the stocks of Honeywell International and Rockwell Automation, major American companies in the automation business, soared over 50% after Trump was elected.

Indian IT companies say they are expanding into cloud-based services and AI. But they will have to compete against Microsoft, Amazon, Oracle and other bigger American companies. If they do so, they risk losing their traditional, and still substantial, IT services contracts with these American companies. Also, there is strong competition from several well-funded, fast growing American start-ups. Palantir Technologies provides software for integrating, visualizing and analyzing data, mainly for intelligence, defense and other security agencies. It is valued at $20 billion. DropBox provides cloud-based storage solutions for Windows, Mac and Linux based systems. It is valued at $9.4 billion.

DocuSign's platform is used for legally compliant digital and electronic signatures in 188 countries and in 43 languages. It went public in 2018 at a valuation of $6.3 billion.

Lessons from Google

Start-ups may have a better chance of success than the larger Indian IT companies in part because they will not be competing with major clients. There are an estimated 300 start-ups pursuing data analytics, AI and other new technologies in India. But like similar start-ups in America, they need major initial investments to hire a group of skilled staff and for equipment and services. This is a big hurdle which was not faced by the earlier generations of internet and software start-ups. Many of the earlier ventures were launched successfully by small teams using their personal savings.

Some of the start-ups in India are pursuing niche markets. Mu Sigma, based in Bangalore and outside Chicago, analyzes data to help Walmart, Pfizer, Dell and other major American companies improve their marketing, risk control and supply chain operations. Revenues reportedly exceeded $180 million in 2017. Founded in 2004, the company has over 3,500 employees, mostly in India. Valued at over $1.5 billion in 2016, it has received $211 million in funding from Sequoia Capital, General Atlantic Partners and MasterCard, according to *Crunchbase*. Founder Dhiraj Rajaram was a consultant at Booz Allen. He has degrees in computer science from Anna University, India, and Wayne State University as well as an MBA from the University of Chicago's Booth school.

In 2017, Google bought Bangalore-based Halli Labs, which seeks to apply machine learning techniques to old problems. Halli's founder Pankaj Gupta worked at Stayzilla, a failed Indian rival to Airbnb, and for five years at Twitter in San Francisco. He has a degree from IIT Delhi and a Ph.D. from Stanford university, both in computer science. In his profile on Linked-in, the online business network, Gupta writes that he is very passionate about "building consumer products that are simple, useful and based on deep tech and data...(and) building great teams that can innovate as well as execute."

Google acquired Halli for an undisclosed amount, less than four months after it was founded. It made the purchase to hire Gupta, according to news reports. After the sale, Gupta moved from Bangalore to San Francisco to become a director of engineering products at Google. Halli was the first business bought by Google in India. Having lost out in China to Chinese competitors, Google and other American companies are aggressively pursuing the Indian market. Overall the strategy of American companies is to make investments and buy start-ups in order to be able to offer new products and services, prevent them from growing into competitors or being acquired by rivals as well as to hire talented staff.

Major Indian IT companies need to follow the example of major American companies if they want to grow their revenues and profits. They should be patient investors in start-ups, willing to accept losses. Most important, Indian companies will have to offer generous financial rewards to attract the top talent. In AI, for instance, Google, Facebook, Microsoft and other technology companies are competing for talent with banks, hedge funds and other companies. Fresh Ph.D.'s in AI, from major American universities, are being paid $300,000 per year. In addition, many of them will get huge financial rewards, through profit sharing and stock options and grants. At Indian IT companies, while founders and a handful of senior managers have gotten wealthy, they do not offer good salaries, bonuses and stock ownership to be able to hire the best talent.

Infosys has a $500 million innovation fund. But at fiscal

year-end 2017, only $45 million was invested in 13 companies. Ratan Tata and some other Indians, including founders of IT companies, are investing in new enterprises, but in their personal portfolio. Since 2012, after retiring as chairman of the Tata Group of companies, Tata has invested in over 30 start-ups in India, including mobile and digital companies like Paytm, a payment service, Ola, a taxi service and rival of Uber, and the retailer Snapdeal. Tata set up RNT Capital which invests in technology start-ups around the world. He is an advisor to Bangalore-based Kalaari Capital as well as IDG Ventures India, which manages $450 million and has invested in over 70 companies.

Kalaari is a Bangalore-based venture fund founded by Indian entrepreneurs and executives returning to India from America. In 2017, Tata spoke at a summit "Billion Aspirations" organized by Kalaari. Explaining his interest, he said that, "I became so excited by what I saw and what I experienced in the startup community — innovation, great passion...it stimulated me. In my years in business, I felt that the companies in India...had been timid in terms of how it addressed the opportunities that existed...India is a large market of growing capability and consumption...the startup activity in the country has been an igniter of passion for thinking big, leading and not following and not being afraid to venture into areas that were considered only available to the big boys."

Chapter 8

INDIA NEEDS MORE ENTREPRENEURS

Up until the 1980's, very few professionals in India pursued entrepreneurship. Romesh Wadhwani says he could not have started his own company in 1969, when he left India to study for a Ph.D. in the U.S. "There was no capital available in India. There was no support...I did not have a business family," Wadhwani told *Forbes.* He is a serial entrepreneur based in America. In 2000, he sold Aspect Development, a software company he founded, for $9.3 billion.

Pioneers from Wipro and Infosys

Indians could raise capital to start a business only if they were backed by a major business family and government officials. A financing chain for start-ups, from angel investors to a stock market listing and private buy-out funds, did not exist. Getting licenses, regulatory and other government approvals was another major hurdle. These processes, controlled by corrupt politicians and bureaucrats, served to protect long-established groups which owned most major Indian businesses. Foreign investors and publications like *The Financial Times* referred to these groups as the Indian oligarchs. They dominated major parts of the economy and prevented competitors from entering their businesses. Professionals in India did not want to give up a job and risk starting a business, fearing they may not find another good job if they fail. Since early childhood they are reminded by parents and others to study hard, do well in the exams, get admitted to a good engineering, medical, management or science college and then find and hold a good job for life.

In 1981, seven graduates of the Indian Institutes of Technology (IIT) pooled together $250 and started Infosys in India. Nandan Nilekani, one of the founders and son of a textile-mill manager, had only $5 in savings when he graduated. Infosys provided low-cost information technology (IT) services to foreign companies. Its first client was Data Basics Corp., an American software solutions company. In fiscal year 2017, Infosys had over $10 billion in global revenues and a market value of $35 billion. Nilekani and the six co-founders are billionaires.

Around the same time as the founding of Infosys, Azim Premji shifted Wipro, his family's $2 million cooking oil business, into providing IT services. The Bangalore-based company has grown into the third largest Indian IT firm with $7.7 billion in revenues in fiscal year 2017. Premji and the founders of Infosys were pioneering professionals turned entrepreneurs. They saw the huge potential market of IT work being outsourced to India, well before major Indian business groups figured it out. The Tata Group was the only major company to move into IT services. In 2017, its Tata Consultancy Services had $18 billion in revenues.

During the 1990's, hundreds of professionals in India became entrepreneurs, mostly in IT and related businesses. This was due to the rapid rise in demand for outsourcing; the Year 2000, or Y2K, issue; cheaper, more powerful communication and IT systems; the initial capital required was small, since the business was based on computer coding skills; and the liberalization and growth in the Indian economy due to reforms started in 1991.

Mobile Internet Creates Billion Dollar Start-Ups

In the 2000s, another wave of IT entrepreneurs emerged in India. More American jobs were outsourced following the recessions of 2000-2002 and 2008-2009. Entrepreneurs in India also benefited from a big inflow of foreign capital. Since 2000, foreign companies and venture and private equity funds have invested over $32 billion in IT and web-based consumer-oriented businesses in India. They want to invest because these businesses are growing rapidly, and that too in a large, expanding market, from which they expect to make huge profits.

Since about 2010, cheaper and improved cellphone services have led to the rapid growth of mobile internet users in India. There are over 400 million smartphone subscribers; and only 24 million homes with landline phones. The rise in mobile internet usage has led to the founding of several businesses which sell products and services online. Some of them are uniquely Indian like Bharatmatrimony and Shaadi, which enable family elders to find wives and husbands for their relatives.

Foreign investors, notably from America and China, have funded much of the rapid growth of mobile-based start-ups in India. In 2017, foreign funds and companies invested about $9 billion in Indian start-ups. Investors include major American funds Sequoia Capital, Tiger Global, Warburg Pincus and General Atlantic Partners, Microsoft, eBay and other American companies as well as Chinese digital giants Alibaba and Tencent Holdings. The Indian operations of Sequoia has raised around $3 billion, making it India's largest venture fund. It has invested in more than 300 start-ups.

Amazon, Google, Facebook and other American companies also continue to invest in their web-based businesses in India. The investors and companies expect to make big gains from the large, rapidly growing demand for retail, taxi-hailing, payments, financial services, video, music, education, healthcare, advertising, social network and other digital services, similar to the gains gotten in the U.S. and China. In 2017, mobile-based businesses in India are estimated to have generated about $120 billion in gross revenues. About a dozen of the start-ups, with good growth, are valued at over a billion dollars. They include taxi-hailing service Ola, mobile payments business Paytm, and data analytics firm Mu Sigma.

Flipkart Founders Become Billionaires

The biggest recent start-up success in India is Flipkart. It was founded by Sachin Bansal and Binny Bansal, who are not related. In 2007, they invested $8,000 of their savings and founded a price comparison site for retail sales on the internet. Flipkart is India's largest online retailer, with an estimated 40% market share. It sells smartphones, electronics, shoes, furniture, apparel, books and other items to over 100 million customers, who shop using their mobile phones.

In 2017, Kalyan Krishnamurthy was appointed chief executive of Flipkart. This change was initiated by Tiger Global, which then owned a third of the company, according to news reports. Krishnamurthy, who is an Indian, had earlier served as the chief financial officer of Flipkart. He was a director of finance and portfolio companies at Tiger Global and had worked at the Asian operations of eBay and Procter & Gamble. He has MBA degrees from the Asian Institute of Management, the Philippines, and UIUC college of business in Illinois, U.S.

Flipkart's gross sales in fiscal year ended March 2018 was $7.5 billion, and net sales $4.5 billion, both up 50% from fiscal 2017. It had accumulated $3.6 billion in losses at year-end 2017. Flipkart raised $7.4 billion in capital, the largest funding for an Indian start-up. Besides Tiger, investors included Microsoft, eBay, venture investor Accel Partners and Naspers, a South African media and technology company. In 2017, the SoftBank Group of Japan bought a 20% stake for $2.5 billion. In May 2018, Walmart said it is buying 77% of Flipkart for $16 billion, valuing the company at $21 billion. The giant American retailer estimates Flipkart's losses will continue into fiscal 2020, mainly due to investments for future growth.

Binny Bansal, Tiger, Microsoft and China's Tencent Holdings will continue as shareholders with Walmart. SoftBank will walk away with a 60% return in about a year. Binny and Sachin Bansal each reportedly own 5% of Flipkart. They will be billionaires when the Walmart transaction closes in late 2018. They are graduates in computer science from the Indian Institute of Technology, Delhi. They first met on the campus, during the summer break of 2005, because they had gotten poor grades and had to finish extra courses in order to be allowed to graduate. Earlier Sachin had failed in his first attempt to get into an IIT. They both grew up in Chandigarh. Sachin comes from a family of agricultural traders while Binny's father was a manager at Punjab National Bank.

Sachin and Binny worked as software engineers in the payments group of Amazon Web Services in Bangalore. Earlier Binny was twice rejected for jobs at Google's Bangalore operations. The financial success of the Bansals, as well as their perseverance despite early failures, will make it easier for Indian parents to accept their children giving up good jobs to start a business. Bhavish Aggarwal, the founder of Ola, told *The Financial Times* that his father did not speak to him for six months, after he started a company that became Ola. In 2010, Aggarwal's father, a doctor, did not want him to give up a job at Microsoft in Bangalore to risk starting his own business. Aggarwal got his engineering graduate from IIT Bombay.

In 2016, Sachin Bansal, the co-founder of Flipkart, told students at IIT, Delhi to pursue business ideas and take risks. Back in 2005, when they were considering launching a business, "entrepreneurship wasn't cool." He said, "I used to regret that I didn't get good grades while at IIT, but I don't regret that anymore." Sachin will leave Flipkart, after the Walmart investment is finalized. His plans include setting up a venture fund to back start-ups in India.

Walmart faces intense competition from Amazon in the American retail market. Its market value is about a third of Amazon's $780 billion. In India, Walmart plans to spend $2 billion to fund Flipkart's growth while Amazon said it will invest $5 billion for its expansion. Flipkart will be a stronger competitor to Amazon in India by adopting Walmart's purchasing, distribution, operations, managerial, technical and other skills. They each have less than 2% share of India's $700 billion consumer retail market. Both Flipkart and Amazon will likely see strong growth, despite their competition, since the market is forecast to grow by about 12% annually for the next several years. Also they offer cheaper and better quality products, due to lower costs from their high volume purchases, efficient supply and distribution systems and not paying rent for physical store locations.

Flipkart and Amazon are also likely to grow much faster in India than the overall market and gain share. Their main competitors are millions of small, independently owned stores, which serve about 90% of the market. The store owners are big supporters and donors to Prime Minister Narendra Modi's party. Their lobbyists are pressuring the government to reject Walmart's investment in Flipkart on grounds of saving jobs. The retail sector employs about 8% of India's labor force. Flipkart and Amazon are creating new jobs. But they have a wide choice of potential employees, given the high unemployment rate. So they may not hire employees fired by small stores who are losing business.

American and Chinese Companies Compete in India

While Tencent of China invested along with American companies and funds in Flipkart, Chinese and American companies are aggressively competing against each other in India. Both of them see India as the major part of their global expansion plans. They are using capital, technology and politics to expand in the market. While Amazon and other major American companies are operating on their own in India, the Chinese have invested over $3 billion in partnership with Indian companies.

In taxi-hailing services, China's Didi Chuxing and Tencent have invested in Ola, founded by an Indian. Ola, valued at $7 billion, faces strong competition from America's Uber, which is valued at $50 billion. In 2015, Alibaba, and its spin-off Ant Financial, invested $680 million in Paytm, India's leading internet-payments company. Alibaba has a market value of $500 billion. The Chinese partner helps with technology, products and market access, Paytm's founder Vijay Shankar Sharma told the *Economic Times*. For instance, using algorithms developed by Alibaba, Paytm has reduced fraudulent transactions to under 0.1%, from about 1%. Alibaba has a good gain on its initial investment. Paytm is valued at about $5 billion.

In 2017, Alibaba invested an additional $200 million in Paytm's web-based retail subsidiary and owns over half of it. Both companies jointly invested $200 million in Bigbasket, at a valuation of about $1 billion. Bigbasket, a digital grocery delivery service operating in several major Indian cities, competes against Amazon. The American magazine *Techcrunch* wrote a story about Alibaba's 2017 investment in Paytm, with the headline: "Its Alibaba versus Amazon in India's e-commerce market."

American web-based companies enjoy very favorable conditions in India as compared to China, the other big market they are pursuing. Facebook and Google, including its YouTube service, do not have access to China. American companies allowed to operate in China face several legal, political, technical and other hurdles. In 2017, for instance, Amazon sold its hardware business for its cloud services in China to a Chinese partner, to comply with local laws. Cloud services is a rapidly growing and highly profitable part of Amazon's business in America. Facebook's messaging app WhatsApp has far fewer users in China than the one billion users on rival WeChat, which is owned by Tencent. The WhatsApp service is censored and has been shut on several occasions by the Chinese government. America's Uber was unable to compete with Didi Chuxing, the market leader in taxi-hailing services. Investors in Didi, which is valued at $56 billion, include major Chinese Internet companies Alibaba and Tencent. In 2016, Uber ended its taxi service in China and merged it with Didi.

Google and Facebook have a more dominant position and greater share of the digital advertising market in India, than they do in America. Facebook has 91% of the market share among India's 160 million social media users, while Google is used for 98% of digital searches, according to *Statcounter*. The American giants are facing rising competition from Chinese companies. Alibaba's UC Browser has a 43% market share among browsers used to access the web through mobile devices in India, according to *Statcounter*. Since it is the operating system on Chinese smartphones, it gives Alibaba control of the gateway to the web use of mobile phone subscribers. The rising popularity of Xiaomi and other Chinese smartphones in India is boosting use of Alibaba's browser. Also, the browser is popular since it uses less memory, blocks advertisements and provides direct links to cricket scores and Bollywood music and news, without users having to click on a search function. Google's Chrome browser is second with a 36% market share.

In 2016, Tencent led a $175 million investment round in Hike, an Indian messaging app. Hike competes against Facebook's

WhatsApp, whose market share in India exceeds 85%. Hike, valued at $1.4 billion, has over 100 million registered users. In 2017, using Tencent's technology, Hike was the first messaging app to launch a mobile payment feature in India, ahead of WhatsApp. The payment method is called blue packets and is similar to the red packets offered by Tencent's WeChat service in China. Hike, founded in 2011 as joint venture between Bharti Airtel and SoftBank, is run by Kavin Mittal. His father is Sunil Mittal, founder of Bharti Airtel which is India's largest telecom services company. The elder Mittal's net worth is estimated to be about $8.1 billion. A *Forbes* story, on the partnership between China's Tencent and Hike, carried the headline: "Tencent Plans to Capture India With the Help of This 29-Year-Old Entrepreneur."

Opportunities in the Old Economy

Indigo is an unusual start-up, operating in an old economy business and set up by an Indian American professional teaming up with business partners in India. In 2006, Rakesh Gangwal joined father and son Kapil and Rahul Bhatia to found the company. Starting with one aircraft, low-cost Indigo has grown into India's largest passenger airline, with 40% of the market share and 168 aircraft. In 1984, after an MBA from the Wharton School, Gangwal began working as a strategic planner for United Airlines. He later worked for Air France and US Airways, where he rose to become the chief executive. Gangwal's 37% ownership of IndiGo gives him a net-worth of $3 billion, according to *Forbes*. He has a degree in mechanical engineering from IIT Kanpur. While Gangwal is based in the U.S., the Bhatias are based in India. The Bhatias have a net worth of $4.3 billion. Rahul got a degree in electrical engineering from the University of Waterloo, Canada.

Healthcare and web-based education are potentially huge markets for entrepreneurs in India. Practo helps patients find doctors, store medical data, order drugs and find healthcare information. The Bangalore-based company has expanded from India to Indonesia, Singapore, Brazil and the Philippines. Its software is licensed by companies in ten countries. Practo was founded by Shashank ND and Abhinav Lal, both graduates of the National Institute of Technology, Karnataka. In 2008, Shashank came up with the idea for the business, after finding it difficult to get a second opinion from a doctor about a knee surgery for his father, according to an opinion piece Shashank wrote for *The Mint*. Practo, valued at over $600 million, has raised $179 million from Sequoia Capital, China's Tencent and other investors.

In education, the total annual revenues of the tutoring business in India, in physical locations as well as online, is estimated to be over $40 billion. One of the successful start-ups in the field is Byju's, which provides fee-based digital tutoring. It uses text, video, animation, chat, quizzes and games to teach math and science to school students and to prepare those taking entrance exams for the IIT's, top management schools, the civil service and other competitive exams.

The company has raised over $240 million in funding, including from the Chan-Zuckerberg Initiative, an investment arm of Facebook founder Mark Zuckerberg and his wife. The Bangalore-based company is valued at $800 million. It was founded in 2011 by Byju Raveendran, a mechanical engineer from the Government College of Engineering in Kerala. "You learn the best when you learn on your own," he told *Quartz*. In 2006, he started by tutoring a group of 40 students, including some of his friends. "I was a teacher by choice and an entrepreneur by chance," he added.

Few Hi-tech Manufacturing Start Ups

While India is a major source of world-class engineering

skills, this is mainly in software and IT services. There are relatively few Indians who have advanced expertise in hardware and manufacturing. This is because India's top engineers are educated mostly in classroom settings. Also, few of them grow up working with and creating gadgets. So there are very few start-ups in high-technology based hardware and industrial businesses.

Prime Minister Narendra Modi sees manufacturing as the key to reducing urban unemployment, which is around 10%. In 2014, soon after he came to power, he announced a "Make in India" policy. The goal is to raise the share of manufacturing to 25% of GDP by 2022, up from about 15%, where it has hovered for decades. Modi expects this would create an additional 100 million jobs. But manufacturing declined slightly in fiscal year 2017, after growing at an average of less than 2% annually from 2011-2016.

Some economists argue that the problems in the growth of manufacturing have to do with the rise of the services sector and the slow growth of the global economy. But there is negligible industrial and manufacturing research and development in the private or public sector or at universities in India. So businesses have to import the latest equipment and technical skills from American, European, Japanese or Chinese companies. Since this requires major capital investments, access to capital becomes the main factor in determining the success or failure of the business. But big commercial banks, burdened with loan losses, are reluctant to lend and charge very high interest rates.

Ather Energy is one of the few Indian high-technology manufacturing start-ups. The Bangalore based company, based in a former rail car manufacturing facility, plans to start selling an electric scooter in late 2018. It will use a lithium-ion battery and travel about 40 miles on a single charge. The retail price is expected to be around $1,500. The company was founded in 2013 by Tarun Mehta and Swapnil Jain, graduates of IIT Madras. Tiger Global, a New York-based fund, invested $12 million in the company. In

2016, Hero MotoCorp, a leading Indian vendor of scooters and motorcycles, committed to invest up to $35 million in Ather. This reportedly gives Hero a roughly 30% ownership stake in the electric scooter start-up.

Grey Orange makes robots which automate the collection and storage of products inside warehouses and distribution and fulfilment centers. The company was started in New Delhi but moved its head office to Singapore. Its research center is based in suburban New Delhi while the robots are assembled in Singapore and China. This is because a supply chain for raw materials does not exist in India, according to a report in the *Financial Times*. Grey Orange was founded in 2011 by Samay Kohli and Akash Gupta, engineering graduates of BITS, India and Wolfgang Hoeltgen, a German seed investor. It got early funding from Tiger Global and Blume Ventures, Mumbai, according to *Crunchbase*.

How to Create 80 Million High-Paying Jobs

Some leading entrepreneurs say that India's should focus on promoting entrepreneurship, not manufacturing. Between 2005 and 2012, while India's GDP grew by 54%, only 15 million, or 3%, net new jobs were created. Also the new jobs, created by small and medium businesses, paid low wages. This giant disconnect will worsen in the future, Romesh Wadhwani wrote in a 2016 opinion article for *The Times of India*. A billionaire serial entrepreneur, he runs U.S. based Symphony Technology Group. It owns 18 technology and other companies, with a combined $2.8 billion in annual revenues.

By 2025, India will add over 80 million net new job seekers, while only 30 million low-wage jobs will be created. The absence of a vibrant, business-oriented research culture has stunted job creation, especially well-paying jobs. Wadhwani says that India needs to build a vast, integrated ecosystem for entrepreneurship education, mentoring and support, in order to create the additional 50 million jobs, which will pay high wages. He adds, "I am a first generation entrepreneur, with no role model for entrepreneurship in my...family. Entrepreneurship is about a state of mind, and about having access to an ecosystem in which startup and growth ideas can be explored..." about education in the basics of startups and small business growth; about access to mentors, innovation funding, angel investors and other sources of capital and support. Vinod Khosla, another Indian American serial entrepreneur and a venture capitalist, also sees entrepreneurs playing a major economic role. In 2013, the billionaire told students at Carnegie Mellon University that "...innovation and entrepreneurship have become important. That's why I believe the power of ideas fueled by entrepreneurial energy is the single most important force in the world for good...I have a lot of disrespect for authority and conventional wisdom, and for expert opinion. I think these are all essential for being an entrepreneur."

Indian government departments should make 500 to 1,000 innovation grants each year to small and medium enterprises, based on competitions organized by the IITs, says Wadhwani. The grants will foster ties between industry and universities and generate quality jobs, similar to what happened in America. Universities should conduct fundamental research as well as find business solutions, he adds. In America, "...the computer industry is a beneficiary of the kind of partnership that can take place between academia and commercial organizations. Most of the interesting advances in computer science have elements of academic research and elements of commercialization that have come together to build great products," noted Bill Gates, then Chief Executive of Microsoft, speaking in 2003 in Cupertino, California, at the 50th anniversary celebration of the IITs.

Nandan Nilekani stresses the important role of small and medium businesses. He is a co-founder of Infosys, India's second largest IT services company. He led the Congress Party government's initiative to provide every Indian with an electronic identity card to enable them to open bank accounts, protect titles to land and home ownership and prevent fraud in the distribution of government-run welfare services. He says that domestic consumption and services need to be boosted. He is critical of Prime Minister Modi's emphasis on exports, manufacturing and large business. In 2016, Nilekani told *The Indian Express*, "I think that manufacturing will not shift from China to India but from China to robots."

Chapter 9

FALLING OIL PRICES BOOST
THE ECONOMY AND MODI

The impact of entrepreneurship on creating jobs and boosting the Indian economy will be far greater if power, transport and other infrastructure is expanded and modernized. So far domestic and foreign private investors have avoided making major infrastructure investments. However they are eagerly pursuing consumer-oriented businesses, which offer prospects for 20% plus annual returns in U.S. dollars due to rapid growth, consumers paying market prices and since there are few government restrictions in such businesses.

One of them is the mobile web-based businesses. Another is pharmaceuticals, where total revenues are forecast to reach $100 billion by 2025. Sales are growing at a compound annual 12% due to a rising population and widespread prevalence of digestive and diarrheal diseases, tuberculosis and diabetes. Also, over 2,600 products and 546 manufacturing plants in India meet the safety standards of the U.S. Federal Drug Administration. Due to this, India is the largest global exporter of generic drugs, including over 80% of the anti-retroviral drugs used to combat AIDS. Exports totaled $17 billion in fiscal 2017. Besides growth, another attraction to foreign companies and funds is that they can own 100% of their Indian pharmaceutical operations. Since 2000, they have invested over $16 billion in the business.

Foreign investors are also pursuing opportunities in the media and entertainment business. Revenues are estimated to grow a compound annual 14%, reaching $38 billion in 2021; up from $20 billion in 2016. Television, which accounts for half of the revenues, is the most lucrative due to rapid growth in advertising and cable and satellite subscriptions. The TV business has attracted most of the $7 billion in foreign investments, since 2000, including from major American companies Disney and 21st Century Fox.

Profits Propel Spread of Mobile Internet Usage

The second biggest foreign investment in India, after mobile web-based consumer businesses, is in telecommunications. It is the success story of the economic reforms first initiated by the Congress Party government in 1991. In early 2018, India had over 400 million mobile smartphone users with internet access, a four-fold increase since 2012. The spread of mobile telecom has created millions of jobs and provided a technological boost to the economy, including enabling the creation of several billion dollar mobile-based businesses.

The private telecom companies benefit from using new, cheaper technologies. They initially competed against inefficient, high cost, government-run operators. In the 2000's, when private companies "...started giving Indians phone connections on demand (versus putting them on a wait-list for years), it was a state duopoly that ceded market share. The government's managers couldn't care less...state-run company hasn't made a single rupee in operating profit in almost a decade," Andy Mukherjee wrote in an opinion column for *Bloomberg* in 2017.

Since 2000, the telecom business has attracted over $24 billion in foreign investments, including $1 billion from Chinese cellphone manufacturers. The private Indian and foreign companies also got $39 billion in cheap loans from Indian government agencies to buy wireless spectrum and equipment, according to *Bloomberg*. In 2017, the retail market for cellphone handsets was about $20 billion. Chinese vendors have captured half the market for smartphones. They have overtaken Samsung and other South Korean suppliers, who have a third of the market. Apple has only a 2% share. Smartphones made by Xiaomi and other Chinese companies are cheaper than those made by Samsung and Apple. India's Reliance Jio is the biggest supplier of feature phones. In 2017, about 70% of the $40 billion revenues of cellular companies came from voice calls. Data services, which accounted for the remaining, are growing rapidly.

Big Potential for Solar Energy

Like the telecom business, solar and wind power systems worldwide are benefitting from new technologies. There is a continuing drop in the prices of equipment and cheaper, more efficient storage systems. In India, solar power has an advantage since the sun rays are strong for several hours a day and there is sunlight for much of the year. Since 2006, solar and wind power generation has risen over five-fold. Together they provide about 8% of India's 330 Gigawatt (GW) of electricity generation capacity.

Renewable energy plants have attracted over $11 billion, mostly from private Indian investors. Many of the wind and solar plants have been funded by companies, commercial and industrial building owners as well as wealthy home owners. They want a reliable source of power which they can control, instead of the erratic supplies and regular black-outs they experience when buying power from government-run utilities. Wipro Ltd, for instance, gets a quarter of its power supply from renewable energy sources. It's a Bangalore-based global information technology services company. Government-run companies are also setting up captive renewable energy plants. The Indian railways, for instance, plans to generate power at train stations using solar panels.

Prime Minister Narendra Modi plans to raise the output of renewable energy, which ties in with his environmental goals. By 2030, he wants to reduce pollution in India, in part by cutting carbon emissions by more than a third. Pollution is an acute, widespread problem, with India ranked at the bottom of a world environmental index, along with Bangladesh and Burundi. The index, prepared by researchers at Yale and Columbia Universities in 2018, measured pollution in air, water, agriculture, fisheries, sanitation and other areas. Also, Delhi and Mumbai were ranked one and four respectively in the World Health Organization's 2018 rankings of large cities with the worst air pollution levels.

Tariffs on Chinese Solar Panels Deters Investors

Coal power plants produce half of India's carbon di-oxide emissions. Modi plans to cut power generation from coal plants by 20%. If it happens, cutting coal consumption will also help reduce India's trade deficit. A fifth of the coal is imported at prices that are twice that of domestic coal. But there is some doubt about India being able to reduce its coal consumption. BP's 2018 Energy Outlook, for instance, forecasts that energy from renewable sources will grow in India over the next two decades. But coal and oil consumption will grow even faster.

By 2022, Modi wants a more than six-fold increase in renewable energy generation to 175 GW, mainly through solar and wind power. He will need to attract over $100 billion in private investments to meet the goal. The government is trying to separate the generation and distribution businesses. This is to try to ensure that the generators are paid for the power they produce and not burdened with the politically difficult task of distributing power and collecting full payments from consumers and farmers. The government is providing land to the operators to set up their plants, helping them overcome a big hurdle in densely populated India. It is also guaranteeing payments in dollars for some projects.

Roughly 300 global and domestic companies plan to invest in renewable power projects in India. They include SoftBank which said it will spend $20 billion to build solar systems. The Japanese company, run by billionaire Masayoshi Son, plans to use part of a $100 billion fund it raised largely from Saudi Arabian and other Persian Gulf government entities. Other investors include EDF Energies, a French electricity company, and Foxconn, the Taiwanese manufacturing company. The government efforts were set back in early 2018, after it imposed 70% tariffs on imports of Chinese solar panels. India does not have the capacity to replace the Chinese panels. The higher cost of setting up solar power plants, resulting from the tariffs on Chinese panels, has dimmed the interest of foreign investors.

Drop in Oil Prices Boosts the Economy

Besides environmental reasons, India needs to expand renewable energy capacity to reduce dependence on crude oil imports and avoid another collapse of the Rupee. In 2013, currency markets were suddenly spooked by India's rising foreign trade deficit. In just four months that year, the Indian Rupee fell sharply by 30% to Rs.69 to a U.S. dollar. The value of the Indian Rupee is tied to the price and volume of crude oil imports, I wrote in an opinion piece for *Knowledge@Wharton*. From 2003 to 2013, while consumption rose sharply, domestic oil production stayed roughly flat, at around 900,000 barrels per day. So, to meet demand, imports quadrupled to a net 2.6 million barrels per day. By 2013, India's oil import bill rose five-fold, due to the rising volume of imports and higher prices, doubling the foreign trade deficit to $196 billion.

Up until 1983, India's automobile industry policies were aimed at restricting oil imports to contain the foreign trade deficit and conserve foreign exchange. In 1980, for instance, only 47,000 cars and 79,000 trucks, buses and vans were sold. Oil imports that year were 600,000 barrels per day and Rs. 10 bought a U.S. dollar. In 1983, automobile production was expanded starting with a joint venture between Maruti, an Indian government-owned company, and Suzuki of Japan. The venture initially assembled Suzuki cars in India from components imported from Japan. It was set up as part of an economic revival plan by Sanjay Gandhi, son of then Prime Minister Indira Gandhi.

Since then major foreign companies, including Ford, Honda and Hyundai, have invested over $16 billion to set up auto plants in India. In fiscal year 2017, automobile sales reached 22 million, including three million cars, over 700,000 commercial vehicles and 18 million scooters and motorcycles. Rising demand for automobiles has boosted oil consumption. About 40% of oil is used for transportation, while manufacturing, especially petrochemicals and oil related products, account for a big portion of the remaining demand. In 2017, net oil imports were 4.3 million barrels per day, two thirds higher than in 2013. Also, India imported roughly half of the five billion cubic feet of natural gas it consumed per day. The price of gas, which is shipped as liquefied natural gas (LNG), is tied to oil prices. In fiscal year 2017, the net import bill for oil, gas and related products fell by half, compared to 2013. This was due to the steep drop in crude oil prices, from $110 per barrel in 2014 to around $50 in 2017.

In the early 2010's, when oil and gas prices were high, farmers, truck owners, businesses and consumers organized protests seeking subsidized prices. The Congress Party government ordered the government-run oil and gas companies to take losses and cut the retail prices for gasoline, diesel, liquefied petroleum gas and other oil and gas based products. The drop in oil prices, from

2014 to 2017, helped the companies to return to profits. It also helped the Modi government reduce the budget and foreign trade deficits as well as stabilized the Rupee. However in 2018, with the rise in oil prices to around $80 a barrel, business and consumer groups are campaigning for cuts in prices. With elections due in 2019, Modi's government is likely to force the government-run oil and gas companies to once again take losses and cut retail prices.

Can Dependence on Oil Imports be Reduced?

In the case of crude oil, India depends on imports for over 80% of its supplies. Proven reserves are estimated to be about 5.5 billion barrels, barely enough to meet four years of consumption. India can reduce its consumption of oil and coal, cutting its import bill as well as pollution, by expanding the use of natural gas. Domestic reserves are large enough to meet future demand: about 43 trillion cubic feet (TCF), with an additional 60 TCF in estimated shale gas reserves.

In 2011, the global energy giant BP paid $7.2 billion for a 30% stake in Reliance Industries' oil and gas fields off the Indian coast. The companies together invested $1.2 billion for exploration and development but gas output from their fields declined sharply. India's total gas output fell to 28 billion cubic meters in 2016, almost half that of 2010. The major exploration and production companies sought higher prices for their gas on grounds that it cost more to produce from difficult regions, such as water depths ranging from 1,200 feet to over 9,000 feet. In 2017, BP and Reliance said they revived their projects and will produce 425 million cubic feet of gas a day within three years. They also expanded their partnership and plan to invest an additional $6 billion for offshore exploration and production. These announcements came a few weeks after Modi's government reportedly allowed companies to get market prices for their gas by selling directly in the domestic market. The government also halved to 5% the royalty payments it charged companies for deep water projects. This led BP and Reliance Industries to withdraw their legal claims against the government, according to news reports.

Modi wants to cut oil imports by 10% through improved road, rail and shipping transportation. By 2030, he wants all new cars to run on electric batteries. He also plans to improve road transport and expand and modernize the more fuel-efficient rail and ship transport systems. About 60% of the goods in India are transported by fuel guzzling, polluting trucks, with an average age of ten years. Their average speed is 13 miles per hour due to congestion and bad roads.

A new highway between Mumbai and Delhi is one of the major projects expected to improve road transportation. When operational, it will reduce a truck's travel time between the cities to 17 hours from 60 hours. The highway is part of a project to develop an industrial corridor between the two major cities. It was launched by the Congress Party government in 2009. The Indian and Japanese governments each pledged to put up 5% of the $100 billion required, expecting to attract private companies to fund the rest. So far private investors have shown little interest in the major road project.

Rail transport and coastal shipping are slow and expensive, pushing shippers to use road transport. India has an extensive government-run rail network with 67,000 miles of tracks, 7,200 stations and 12,600 passenger and 7,400 freight trains operating each day. But freight trains, which move three million tons of cargo a day, run at an average speed of 15 miles per hour. In fiscal 2017, the rail network lost about $5 billion on $26 billion in revenues, mainly since the rates charged for freight transport are far below cost. It is hence not surprising that, up until 2016, foreign companies and funds had invested only $790 million in businesses tied to the rail network.

Prime Minister Modi is offering several incentives to lure GE, Alstom and major Japanese and German companies as well as Indian private companies to invest over $140 billion for the expansion and modernization of the rail network. In 2017, work started on a bullet train project to connect Mumbai and Ahmedabad. It is being funded by a $14 billion, 50 year loan at 0.1% annual interest from the Japanese government. The operator expects to cover costs by pricing tickets much higher than airline fares between the two Western Indian cities. Critics say the money should have been spent on upgrades, especially installing electronic signals to improve safety and speed. They also say that it's unlikely that Japan will recoup its investment. But the goal of the Japanese appears to be to win other, more lucrative contracts in the future.

In shipping, India's 4,500 mile coastline has 13 major and 64 smaller ports. There are both private and government-run shipping companies. From 2000 to 2016, foreign companies invested only $1.6 billion in shipping and ports facilities. Since 2014, Modi has changed the rules to permit private companies to fully own port facilities, which they construct and maintain. He has also granted a 10 year tax holiday to foreign investors. By 2022, Modi expects these and other incentives will attract over $65 billion from private companies. His plan calls for tripling the port capacity to over three billion tons per year, through upgrades, expansions and development of an additional eight major ports.

Chapter 10

SEEKING $500 BILLION IN
FOREIGN CAPITAL

In 2014, many Indian and Western economists and journalists eagerly welcomed Prime Minister Narendra Modi saying he would usher in an era of rapid economic growth. But, more than four years later, his policies have had little impact on growth. In fiscal year ended March 2018, gross domestic product (GDP) grew by 6.7%. The best year under Modi was fiscal 2015 when GDP grew by 7.9%. But, as economists have pointed out, roughly two percent of the growth that year - and in 2016 - was due to the boost from a decline in crude oil prices. In fiscal 2014, under the previous Congress Party government, GDP grew by 6.6%.

A Near Bankruptcy Forces Economic Reforms in 1991

Up until the 1980's, India was a statist, centrally directed and regulated economy. "Transport, agriculture and construction sectors were owned and administered by the Central Government, commodity prices were regulated and the country had important trade barriers," note Lucas Chancel and Thomas Piketty in a 2017 research paper. In 1991, loans from the International Monetary Fund (IMF) saved India from a severe foreign currency shortage which almost bankrupted the country. As part of the bailout, the

125

IMF forced India to reduce import duties for some goods, from over 110% to under 40%, permit foreign investments in more business areas and allow private companies to operate in the insurance and telecommunications businesses. Up until then, these were reserved exclusively for government-run companies.

Setting up a new business in India became easier. But this change mainly benefitted major multinational corporations and hurt Indian companies. The Tata Group, sensing the shift, started expanding abroad in 1992 "...one year after the Indian government lifted foreign investment and exchange controls and eliminated many restrictions on outside companies. Suddenly, multinationals such as Sony, Philips, Ford, and Toyota entered India, exposing the quality problems of many local companies and using their marketing prowess to outpace popular domestic players like Tata," writes Ann Graham in "Too good to fail", an article about the Tata Group. It was published in 2010 by Booz Allen, a consulting firm, in its *Strategy+Business*. The article is also posted on Tata's website. The Tata group controls over a hundred different businesses, ranging from salt and tea to steel and cars. It has over 700,000 employees in its global operations.

"Before the 1990s, when Indian businesses were protected from outside competition but also limited by tight government controls, Tata's domestic expansion and diversification positioned the group as one of the two or three largest companies in India," Graham writes. Since 1992, the group found it easier to grow profitably outside India, than compete within the country. Tata's foreign investments are based on a strategy of seeking prestigious consumer brands and critical industrial businesses and include Jaguar, Land Rover and Tetley Tea. In fiscal year 2017, two thirds of the group's $100 billion in revenues came from outside India.

Many Indian and western economists and journalists forecast that the liberalization would generate rapid growth, pushing India's economy to become larger than China's in twenty years. But till recently, India's growth was less than half that of China's. India's gross domestic product is less than a quarter of China's $11.2 trillion. India's share of world trade in goods and services is 2.2%, while that of China is 10.1%. The average Indian's per capita income is $1,700 per year, while that of a Chinese is $6,800. The poverty rate in China is below 10%, while it is more than double that in India. The Chinese on average live a decade longer than Indians.

Cancellation of High Value Notes

Since becoming Prime Minister in 2014, Narendra Modi has introduced several useful reforms, though there were problems with implementing some of them. In 2016, he cancelled high value currency, which then totaled about 80% of the $240 billion of notes in physical circulation. His officials predicted this demonetization would reduce tax evasion and corruption. In fiscal year 2018, only 61 million citizens, or under 5% of the population, filed personal income taxes. In levels of corruption, India ranks 81 among all countries, behind China and South Africa, according to Transparency International. The Berlin-based organization, with chapters in over 100 countries, is a non-profit that gives a voice to "victims and witnesses of corruption."

Modi's demonetization hurt the poor and middle classes. They could not afford to wait in line for days at banks to exchange the old notes for the new ones. With India being a cash-based economy and since they needed quick cash, they were forced to sell the cancelled notes to money lenders at discounts to face value of up to 30%. The money lenders were reportedly able to convert the cancelled notes into new legal ones, by bribing bank and government officials.

Modi's officials expected that a third of the demonetized currency would vanish since tax cheaters and corrupt officials would be unwilling to disclose their wealth. But a 2017 report by the Reserve Bank of India showed that nearly 99% of the high value, cancelled notes were deposited in banks. Critics say that this shows that the policy helped illegal money become legal. The government says it is continuing with plans to identify and prosecute the tax evaders and the corrupt. It is investigating 1.8 million bank accounts of individuals and companies whose cash deposits after demonetization were far larger than the income they reported on their tax filings. Modi will get a popular boost if his government prosecutes even a small fraction of these tax-evading account holders.

A New Tax Collection System

In 2017, Modi's government set up a new online tax collection system in part to reduce tax evasion by businesses. India has one of the worst tax-to-GDP ratios at 17%, compared to even other large emerging countries. It is 26% for South Africa and 32% for Brazil. India also ranks 172/190 in terms of the ease of paying taxes. The new system in India, a nationwide Goods and Services Tax, replaced a value added tax and a complex web of other state and local taxes. It requires businesses with revenues of over $31,000 to upload their invoices each month to an online government portal. The invoices of a business are electronically matched with those of its suppliers and vendors, who also have to upload their invoices to claim tax credits. This is expected to improve tax collection due to peer to peer pressure.

The electronic process has done away with the physical collection of taxes at state and city borders, sharply reducing the transit time for trucks. Also in the fiscal year ended March 2018, there was an 18% jump in income taxes collected due to a 25% jump in the number of personal income tax filers. This was due to the impact of both the demonetization and the new tax system.

Modi has also passed laws to clean up the cheating, corruption and money-laundering in the real estate industry. For instance, developers are prohibited from shifting funds from one project to a different project. In the past, this left buyers waiting for years to get their apartments. Developers fund projects by taking deposits from buyers, which are often up to 30% or more of the total value of the apartment.

A $2 billion Bank Fraud

In February 2018, Punjab National Bank said that a diamond dealer and his business colleagues allegedly defrauded it of $2 billion. The government-owned institution is the second largest bank in India. The fraud, using forged documents, started in 2011. It was allegedly carried out with the help of corrupt bank officials. The bank's stock dropped 60%, following the disclosure.

The diamond dealer Nirav Modi, with retail outlets in New York, London, Hong Kong, Beijing and Mumbai, was a jeweler to Hollywood and Bollywood stars. In 2017, Modi's company claimed sales of over $2.3 billion. *Forbes* estimated his net worth that year to be $1.8 billion, ranking him 85th on its list of 1,234 Indian billionaires. According to his business website, Modi is an art collector who handcrafts rare diamond jewelry using innovative processes and utmost precision.

Modi's company filed for bankruptcy in a New York court and he is reportedly seeking asylum in the U.K. The diamond dealer is unrelated to Prime Minister Modi. In 2017, the Indian government initiated court proceedings in the U.K. to extradite Vijay Mallya to face fraud and money laundering charges in India. His Kingfisher Airlines faced growing losses and shut down in 2012, failing to repay $1.3 billion in loans to Indian banks. Mallya moved to the United Kingdom.

$146 Billion in Bad Loans at Banks

Nirav Modi's and Mallya's bank frauds are not isolated problems. In 2017, figures compiled by the Reserve Bank of India (RBI) showed that businesses had cumulatively defaulted or stopped payments on about $146 billion in loans. Prime Minister Modi's government has passed laws to speed up the bankruptcy process and the recovery of bad loans. It has enabled the RBI to seize bankrupt companies from defaulting owners in nine months, sell the business and distribute the proceeds to creditors. New laws also allow any significant creditor to institute insolvency proceedings against a defaulting company and to get the dispute resolved in 18 months, through liquidation if necessary. Any entity in default for more than a year, or anyone connected with them, is barred from the auction of bankrupt companies.

Yet at the same time, Modi and his ministers are not hiring independent officials who can implement the policies. The most visible example was the failure to re-appoint Raghuram Rajan as head of the RBI. In 2013, Rajan was appointed to lead the central bank by the previous Congress Party government. A professor at the University of Chicago, he was earlier the IMF's chief economist. As head of the RBI, Rajan tried to get the government to improve the scrutiny of its banks and their loans. He forced the government-run banks to disclose about $40 billion in bad loans. He then pressured them to find ways to recover the loans from the defaulting businesses. In 2016, economists at global investment banks as well as editorials in business publications urged Modi to re-appoint Rajan for a second term. But Modi did not do so, apparently under pressure from business groups affected by Rajan's measures. Most of the bad loans are owed by major privately owned companies.

Government-run companies, which operate most of India's infrastructure businesses, have accumulated an additional $20 billion plus in losses. This is due to government mandated policies like charging prices below costs and hiring excess staff. Modi's officials are pushing the loss-making government-run companies to become profitable or be sold. In fiscal 2017, the government raised $5 billion from a partial sale of its stakes in several companies. The buyers of the stock offerings were other government-run companies like banks and insurers, according to a report in *The Hindu*. There were no private investors risking their funds, who would try to clean up the operations and make the businesses profitable.

Seeking Western Investors for Infrastructure Projects

Bad loans accounted for 13% of total bank lending outstanding. Most of them are owed to government-run banks, which account for two-thirds of the nation's bank assets. These banks are the main source of domestic capital for businesses in India. But in fiscal 2017, new loan growth was 5%, the slowest increase in over six decades, according to RBI data. The banks are investing in government debt, instead of making loans and risking more losses. Also, in fiscal 2018, India's budget deficit was 3.5% of GDP. The losses at the government-run banks and companies and the budget deficits severely restricts Modi's ability to fund major infrastructure and development projects.

His government needs to attract over $500 billion in foreign capital to meet his economic goals. India is an attractive market, even when compared to China, for American, Japanese and European investors. It has a large, growing population, half of them under the age of 25. Unlike in China, foreign companies are not forced to share their technology and intellectual property with Indian partners, who could be potential rivals. Also, foreign investors and companies can easily move their capital and profits out of India in dollars.

Contracts with private Indian companies can be enforced, especially if signed under American or European law and the Indian companies own assets in the U.S. or Europe. Also, unlike in China, foreign companies and investors can apply pressure on errant Indian companies through diplomatic channels and the Indian government. The Indian government can be pressured to force Indian companies to meet contractual obligations as well as open up markets. This is because India needs foreign capital and technology and imports much of its defense equipment.

Legacy of Enron's Power Plant Disaster

Since assuming office over four years ago, Modi has attracted only a small amount of foreign funds needed, despite introducing investor friendly policies and incentives. Typically Western investors seek a minimum 10% annual real return in U.S. dollars for infrastructure investments in developing countries; slightly less if the government guarantees a return. In India, they are waiting to see if the early, smaller projects earn good returns. They also recall that major losses were incurred by those who previously invested in Indian infrastructure projects.

In the 1990's, private domestic and foreign companies and funds eagerly invested in an equally ambitious infrastructure plan pursued by the then Congress Party government. In the power area, for instance, big American and European companies were given secret "fast track" approvals to set up eight major plants. The biggest of them was a $3 billion, 2,500 Megawatt power plant in Dabhol, Maharashtra, to be set up by Enron. The American energy company and the other companies raised several billion dollars, including in dollar denominated debt partly guaranteed by the Indian and foreign governments.

Ignoring legal contracts, Indian officials did not permit the companies to raise electricity prices, especially for farmers and consumers. The companies also lost power to theft and unauthorized use. Seven of the plants failed due to cost overruns and losses. The investors abandoned the projects and launched law-suits against the Indian government. In 2001, the Enron plant was shut due to numerous legal and technical issues. It was restarted five years later under the ownership of two government-run power companies.

The Dabhol debacle had its seamier side. It appears that Enron was only interested in the Indian power plant as a buyer for the liquefied natural gas it was planning to produce in Qatar. The World Bank refused to fund the power project saying it was economically unfeasible. In 2001, Enron tried unsuccessfully to sell the plant and other foreign operations, just before it filed for bankruptcy. There were allegations that the company bribed Indian officials to clear farmers from their land and to harass and arrest those protesting the setting up of the plant. In a 2002 report, Human Rights Watch said that "Enron was complicit in human rights abuse in India for several years."

Chapter 11

RISK OF RADICALIZING INDIA'S
180 MILLION MUSLIMS

Some economists and analysts argue that Prime Minister Narendra Modi is a pragmatist, focused on growing India's economy and its global stature. So they say western investors should ignore the Hindu extremist agenda of his Bharatiya Janata Party (Indian People's Party) (BJP) as a minor political distraction. But western companies and funds, investing in long-term infrastructure and development projects, seek countries which are not facing potentially widespread, violent internal conflicts. One major reason for Modi being unable to meet his economic goals "has to do with the increasing power of sectarian Hindu factions, which are beginning to erode India's openness, tolerance of minorities and freedom of press," Kaushik Basu wrote in the *Financial Times,* in 2017. Small traders, informal workers as well as big corporations are fearful and sense social deterioration, he adds. Basu is a professor of economics at Cornell University. Earlier he was the chief economist of the World Bank and, from 2009 to 2012, he was an economic adviser to the Congress Party government in India. Kaushik Basu has a Ph.D. in economics from the London School of Economics.

A Hindu Warrior-Priest heads a State Government

In 2014, soon after Modi became Prime Minister, a senior leader of his party told *The Guardian* that India would be "a power with dignity, with responsibility...for all Indians." But Modi has remained silent while Hindu extremists have attacked Muslims and Christians. In 2017, after his party won the elections in Uttar Pradesh (U.P.,) Modi appointed Yogi Adityanath as head of the state government. Yogi is a warrior-priest and head of a militant, Hindu supremacist temple. A video of one of his campaign speeches on YouTube shows him rousing supporters by saying that if Muslims kill one Hindu man, "then we will kill 100 Muslim men." Yogi has an army of 250,000 vigilante volunteers, organized to the village level. Commenting on why Yogi was appointed head of the state government, *The Economist* pointed out that Modi's Hindu nationalist base, "have lent their vast numbers and organizational genius to Mr. Modi's electoral machine. Now they want their pound of flesh."

Yogi promised to strictly enforce a ban on cow slaughter, if his party was elected. Cows are sacred to the Hindus. The first act of Yogi's government was to shut down several abattoirs and meat shops in the state, without providing any evidence of their killing cows. Thousands of Muslims and low-caste Hindus lost their jobs and the business owners and Hindu buffalo farmers suffered losses. Half of the beef produced in India comes from U.P. The abattoirs and retail meat shops are owned by Muslims. They buy buffalos from Hindu dairy farmers. The animal skins are bought by tanneries and leather goods businesses owned by Muslims and low-caste Hindus. Their workers are low-caste Hindus and Muslims. In addition to such close business links, leaders of the Muslims, the Hindu dairy farmers and low-caste Hindus have often allied together to win elections in the state.

In 2007, Yogi was imprisoned for provoking violence

against Muslims by Mulayam Singh Yadav, then head of the U.P. government. Earlier in 1990, Lalu Prasad Yadav, head of the government in Bihar, halted a march by Hindu extremists which was on its way to destroy a mosque and replace it with a temple. Lalu jailed the leader of the march who was from Modi's party. Mulayam and Lalu are leaders of Yadav's, a Hindu sub-caste of dairy farmers. They are major suppliers of buffalos to the beef abattoirs owned by the Muslims.

Hindus & Muslims Benefit from Sales of Buffalo Beef

Livestock farming is a $100 billion business, about a quarter of India's agricultural gross domestic product. In fiscal year 2017, about 138 million tons of milk were produced by water buffalos and cows. The sale of meat from buffalos, goats, sheep, chickens and pigs is legal, while killing cows is illegal. Meat is eaten by Muslims, Christians and Sikhs; most Hindus are vegetarians. In 2017, five million tons of buffalo beef were produced in India. Revenues from the beef and leather industries totaled about $18 billion that year.

In 2017, two million tons of beef were exported, a fourteen-fold increase over the previous decade. India is the world's largest beef exporter, with Vietnam being a major buyer. The exporters run mechanized slaughter-houses which meet high sanitary standards and pass regular quality inspections from the foreign buyers. Major western brands such as Tommy Hilfiger, Zara and Marks & Spencer source some of their leather goods from India. In 2017, beef exports were $5 billion and leather goods exports were $6 billion. If added together, they covered two thirds of India's foreign trade deficit in that year.

Since the 2000s, the rapid growth of the beef and leather businesses have generated much-needed jobs for Muslims and low-caste Hindus. The beef industry employs about five million people, mostly Muslims, while the leather business employs an additional three million, Muslims and low-caste Hindus. At the same time, millions of Hindu dairy farmers are earning higher incomes by raising more buffalos. Several Muslims and low-caste Hindus have prospered by owning beef and leather businesses. Prime Minister Modi's goal is to more than triple the output and exports of beef and leather goods by 2022, according to government statements. The biggest obstacle to achieving this goal is his party's aggressive pursuit of a Hindu extremist agenda.

Hindu-Muslim Clashes to win Votes

The electoral strategy of Modi's party is to get Hindu votes by accusing Muslims of killing cows and Hindu political opponents of protecting the cow-killers. The most effective weapon used by Hindu extremists is to provoke bloody Hindu-Muslim clashes and then campaign as protectors of the Hindus. (For a discussion of this strategy see Appendix C.) Since 1999, Yogi's vigilantes were reportedly involved in at least 22 major Hindu-Muslim clashes and numerous minor ones. Yogi often magnified petty matters, such as spitting on the streets, to provoke attacks on Muslims, reports *The Business Standard*. The Muslims fear Yogi's vigilantes. "If you talk too much, we will kill you," the vigilantes tell the Muslims, *The New York Times* reported.

In 2012, a coalition of political parties representing Yadav's and low-caste Hindus as well as Muslims defeated Modi's party in the state elections in U.P. A year later, it was too much of a coincidence that major clashes broke out between Hindus and Muslims in the state. About 60 people were killed, mostly Muslims. The clashes in 2013, and a series of other Hindu-Muslim clashes triggered by Hindu extremists, helped Modi's party win subsequent elections in the state in two major ways.

First, in the 2014 national elections, Modi's party won most of the seats in U.P. because it got the support of some from the Hindu farmer caste. Sanjeev Balyan emerged as a local leader of Modi's party during the clashes in 2013. He won election to parliament because he rallied the Jats to attack Muslims, according to news reports. The Jats are a Hindu farmer sub-caste in UP and other Hindi speaking states. They traditionally voted for parties led by Jat leaders, some of whom allied with Muslim leaders. Balyan, a veterinarian, is a junior minister in Prime Minister Narendra Modi's government.

Second, fewer Muslims supported the Yadav party in U.P. in the 2014 national and 2017 state elections. They were upset at the Yadav party-led government, which ruled the state from 2012 to 2017, for not protecting them during the 2013 clashes as well as not compensating them for their loss of property. Over 40,000 Muslims fled their homes during the clashes. It is likely that most of their land, homes and other property were stolen by local gangsters, operating as Hindu extremist leaders. This economic aspect of many Hindu-Muslim clashes is vividly shown in *Garam Hawa* (Scorching Winds,) a Hindi film by M.S. Sathyu. It is a story about Hindu criminals destroying the leather business of a Muslim and taking over his large family house. In 1947, after the partition of India and Pakistan, the Muslim small businessman decided to continue living in a northern Indian town, unlike others in his family who had fled to Pakistan.

23 Muslims Lynched During Modi's Rule

Since Narendra Modi became Prime Minister in 2014, at least 23 Muslims and four low-caste Hindu men have been lynched and over 200 injured. They were attacked by Hindu mobs over unproven rumors that they had killed cows or sold or ate cow meat. In two cases the mobs hung the victims, while in two others they stripped, chained and beat the men, says a 2017 report by

IndiaSpend, a Mumbai-based non-profit data resource for journalists. The lynch mobs were led by local leaders of Modi's party and Hindu extremist groups, according to reports. "Vigilante cow-protection groups associated with nationalist Hindu organizations" engaged in a number of assaults on Muslims and low-caste Hindus, according to the 2017 report by Freedom House. "Prime Minister Narendra Modi has been criticized for failing to promptly condemn the attacks," the report added. Freedom House, founded in 1941 and based in Washington D.C., is an independent watchdog dedicated to the expansion of freedom and democracy.

The New York Times, The Guardian, The Washington Post, the *BBC,* other western media and civil rights groups regularly report about the lynching in India. For instance, the 2018 Human Rights Watch report noted that vigilante mob attacks on Muslims, by groups affiliated with the ruling BJP and other Hindu extremist organizations, continued amid rumors that they sold, bought, or killed cows for beef. Instead of taking prompt legal action against the attackers, police frequently filed complaints against the victims under laws banning cow slaughter. Modi's government failed "to promptly or credibly investigate the attacks, while many senior BJP leaders publicly promoted Hindu supremacy and ultra-nationalism, which encouraged further violence," the report continued. In July 2017, the report added, "an affiliate organization of the BJP, the Rashtriya Swayamsevak Sangh" (RSS) (National Volunteer Organization,) announced plans to recruit 5,000 religious soldiers to control cow smuggling and love jihad.

Up until 2017, influential business publications in the West assumed that Modi would keep his word as Prime Minister and treat India's secular constitution as his "bible." In 2014 for instance, *The Economist* carried a story "Why India's Muslims are so moderate." It noted that Indian Muslims have reasons to be upset since "they endure lower levels of education, income, political representation or government jobs than the majority Hindus." Yet

Muslims have remained moderate, the weekly added, due to integration with Hindus, a secular constitution and targeted welfare programs.

Rising Criticism of Modi in the Western Media

Since 2017, widely publicized lynching of innocent Muslims and the appointment of Yogi as head of the UP state government has alarmed the western business media. Ten Muslims were lynched that year. In one case, an argument broke out between some Hindu passengers and a sixteen-year-old Muslim over a seat on a train near Delhi. The Muslim teenager was called a "beef eater," stabbed several times and then thrown off the running train. "When I reached the spot, my (elder) son was sitting on the station with (my younger son's) body soaked in blood in his lap," his father told *The Hindustan Times*. "He was a child. How could they hate us so much to have killed him so brutally?"

In Rajasthan, a Muslim man was killed with an iron pick-axe and his body burnt. A video of the killing, recorded on a smartphone by the alleged killer's nephew, went viral. The killer says he attacked the Muslim because he was "roaming around" with a Hindu girl and to protect Hindus from "love jihad." The term has been popularized "by radical Hindu fringe groups, who accuse Muslim men of participating in a 'conspiracy' to turn Hindu women from their religion by seducing them," the *BBC* reported. Earlier in 2017, two other Muslim men were killed in the state. One of them was killed by Hindu vigilantes claiming to protect cows. He named six of his killers before he died, but the police did not prosecute any of them, according to *The Wire*.

Business publications, including *The Economist, The Financial Times* and *The Wall Street Journal,* are increasingly critical of Modi's appeasement of Hindu extremists and his neglect of economic goals. A long report in *The Wall Street Journal* carried the headline "Modi's Illiberal New India – His Hindu nationalism reigns in politics, media and culture." An editorial in *The Economist* raised doubts about Modi being more committed to economic development than his party's Hindu agenda. In 2002, Modi was chief minister of Gujarat when over 2,000 people, most of them Muslims, were killed in riots there. Modi "has never categorically condemned the massacre or apologized for failing to prevent it," the weekly pointed out. These killings in Gujarat "…were not inchoate mob violence, triggered by real or rumored insult; rather, they involved careful planning by organized Hindu extremists with an explicit program and a developed religious-nationalist ideology," Paul Marshall noted in a report for the Hudson Institute, a conservative research foundation based in Washington D.C.

The western media coverage of the lynching of Muslims, as well as attacks on foreign women tourists, are hurting tourism. A Google search for popular tourist destinations in India, instead brought up a post by a traveler titled "Is India a dangerous place to visit?" The post, on the influential travel website *TripAdvisor*, showed up on the first page of the search results, indicating that it was widely read.

Wealthier Americans and British account for over 20% of foreign visitors. In fiscal year 2018, they are estimated to have spent more than a third of the $28 billion in foreign exchange earned by the tourism business. The business will collapse if Hindu extremists physically damage the Taj Mahal, the top destination for foreign tourists. Some leaders of Modi's party have organized religious protests at the Taj, saying it's a "blot on Indian culture built by traitors." In 2017, funding for the upkeep of the monument, which is located in the state of U.P., was abolished by Yogi's government. Rajasthan, with its red sandstone palaces and luxurious lake hotels in Udaipur, Jaipur and Jaisalmer, is very popular with American tourists. Three Muslims were lynched in the state in 2017.

Fear of Radicalized Muslims

The rise in lynching is making it more difficult for Modi to attract the $500 billion in foreign investments needed to achieve his economic development and job creation goals. Strong media criticism is causing nervousness among boards of foreign corporations and funds which are considering investing in India. This is especially true among American and Western European institutions where boards face close media and public scrutiny over the ethical consequences of their investments. More important, on the business side, western executives and fund managers are asking if the lynching will lead to regular outbreaks of widespread violence and thereby cause major economic disruptions.

The big fear among Western analysts and journalists is that the rise in lynching, combined with a lack of education and jobs, raises the risk that radical Islamic groups could find recruits for terrorist actions. There are about 180 million Muslims in India. More than a third of them live in poverty, twice the national average. They have the lowest level of education among all religious groups. The illiteracy rate among Muslims is 43%, while it is 36% for Hindus. Half the Muslim women are illiterate. Also, fewer than three percent of Muslims have college degrees, which is less than half the level of that of other Indians.

One in five educated Muslim youth is unemployed, while the unemployment among the uneducated is far higher. Three out of four Muslims, who have formal jobs, work for the government, mostly in low-level positions. But after Modi came to power, some government departments have stopped hiring Muslims. Most Muslim men work in informal, low-skill jobs as butchers, bakers and laborers and repair umbrellas, stoves and other simple gadgets. Some Muslim women find work as cooks, baby sitters and house cleaners in middle-and upper-class homes. There are several hundred thousand Indian Muslims, mostly men from Kerala and Tamil Nadu, working in Saudi Arabia, Kuwait and other Persian Gulf countries.

So far there have been isolated cases of major terrorist attacks by Islamic radicals in India. Many of these attacks occurred in Mumbai, India's commercial capital. In 1993, bomb blasts killed over 250; in 2003, over 50 died in car bomb blasts; and in 2006, over 200 were killed in bomb blasts on suburban trains. India's neighbor Pakistan, where over 95% of the population is Muslim, provides sanctuary and support for radical Islamic groups. The countries have fought three wars. Over the past several decades, Islamic groups have launched violent attacks on the police, army and civilians in India, from bases in Pakistan. The criminals who organized the 1993 bomb blasts in Mumbai fled to Pakistan. Bangladesh, India's neighbor on the east, also has a predominantly Muslim population. Since 2013, over 20 intellectuals, journalists, bloggers and foreigners have been killed, including by beheadings, by radical Islamic groups in Bangladesh.

In 2017, Rahul Gandhi pointed to the risk of radicalization, while speaking to students at the University of California, Berkeley. The leader of the Congress Party said that "…people being lynched because they are Dalits (low-caste Hindus), Muslims killed on suspicion of eating beef, this is new in India and damages India very badly. The politics of hate divides and polarizes India making millions of people feel that they have no future in their own country. In today's connected world, this is extremely dangerous. It isolates people and make them vulnerable to radical ideas."

Chapter 12

WILL THE OPPOSITION UNITE TO DEFEAT MODI IN 2019?

Hindus who criticize Hindu extremists are also facing attacks. In September 2017, Gauri Lankesh was shot dead outside her home in Bangalore, India's silicon valley. She was a journalist, who wrote in both English and Kannada, the language of Karnataka. She was a Hindu who was critical of Hindu extremism. "Let us say it loud and clear. Hindu terror units killed Gauri Lankesh," her lawyer told *The Hoot*, a non-profit seeking to promote freedom and independence of the media in India. "Wherever there was communal violence against Muslims, against dalits (low-caste Hindus) or hatred being spread, she would go there," the lawyer added. A week before she was killed, Lankesh told a columnist for *The Wire*, a digital publication, "Those who understand technology are silent. I will do what I can and I will say what I should. These intolerant voices find strength in our silence. Let them learn to argue using words instead of threats." After Lankesh's murder, Siddharth Bhatia, a founding editor of *The Wire* tweeted, "The message and not to independent journalists but to all dissenters is loud and clear. We are watching you and one day we will get you."

Attacks on Civil Liberties and the Media

In 2017, eleven journalists were killed in India. The country ranks 136 out of 192 on the World Press Freedom Index. Media freedom in India ranks behind that in Afghanistan, Angola, Zimbabwe, Myanmar and Cambodia. "Journalists are increasingly the targets of online smear campaigns by the most radical nationalists, who vilify them and even threaten physical reprisals," the 2017 Freedom Index report notes. Compiled annually by Reporters Without Borders, the index measures the level of media freedom in a country. It is an independent organization founded in 1985, which is a consultant to the United Nations.

Other reputed global civil liberties groups also point to the rising threats to democracy posed by the Hindu extremists. According to a Human Rights Watch report, "...vigilante violence aimed at religious minorities, marginalized communities, and critics of the government - often carried out by groups claiming to support the ruling Bharatiya Janata Party - became an increasing threat in India in 2017. Dissent was labeled anti-national, and activists, journalists, and academics were targeted for their views, chilling free expression."

"Prosecutions are also used to gag journalists who are overly critical of the government..." with threats of punishments by life imprisonment, notes Reporters Without Borders. In June 2017, government agents raided the offices of NDTV, a television channel. The agents were investigating a bank loan taken by the company in 2008 and repaid the next year, according to news reports. The TV channel is also under investigation for alleged non-payment of tax liabilities and raising funds abroad. NDTV is one of the few influential media outlets in India that seeks to cover news with impartiality, giving equal time to Modi's government and its critics. NDTV said the investigation was part of the harassment it faces from the government. NDTV "had closely investigated sectarian (Hindu-Muslim) riots in Gujarat that occurred while Modi was its chief minister in 2002, and which human rights groups say his government ignored or abetted," Sevanti Ninan, editor of *The Hoot*, told *The Guardian*.

In addition to physical and legal threats, Modi's party is also using financial incentives to buy support for his government and party. "India's big media conglomerates are either owned by fans of the BJP," or reliant on advertising revenues from government and government run institutions, *The Economist* noted. Also, "with Hindu nationalists trying to purge all manifestations of 'anti-national' thought from the national debate, self-censorship is growing in the mainstream media," the Freedom Index report notes.

Censoring a Nobel Prize Winner

School and college text books are being re-written to conform with the ideology of Hindu extremism. There is growing scrutiny and censorship of the work of academics. In 2017, a documentary about Nobel Prize winner and Harvard economist Amartya Sen's book *The Argumentative Indian*, was denied a license for public screenings in India. The film certification board wanted the film maker to delete words like "cow," "Hindu India," "Hindutva" (Hindu nationalism) and "Gujarat," a state whose government was headed by Modi before he became Prime Minister. Sen's book "...dwells (rather ironically) on India's long history of intellectual pluralism and public debate," *The Washington Post* reported. Sen is a Bengali and a Hindu. "If somebody of his (Sen's) stature cannot express himself freely, what hope does the common citizen have," tweeted Mamta Banerjee, head of the government of West Bengal. She is a Hindu who opposes Prime Minister Modi's Hindu extremist agenda.

Sen describes the horrors faced by the poor during Hindu-

Muslim clashes, in his biography posted on the website of the Nobel Prize committee: "I had to observe, as a young child (in the 1940s,) some of that mindless violence. One afternoon in Dhaka, a man came through the gate screaming pitifully and bleeding profusely. The wounded person, who had been knifed on the back, was a Muslim daily labourer, called Kader Mia. He had come for some work in a neighbouring house - for a tiny reward - and had been knifed on the street by some communal thugs in our largely Hindu area. As he was being taken to the hospital by my father, he went on saying that his wife had told him not to go into a hostile area during the communal riots. But he had to go out in search of work and earning because his family had nothing to eat. The penalty of that economic unfreedom turned out to be death, which occurred later on in the hospital. The experience was devastating for me, and suddenly made me aware of the dangers of narrowly defined identities..."

India has had democratically elected governments for 70 years, except for a state of emergency from 1975 to 1977. (See Appendix D.) Civil liberties, a free media and respect for all religions are among the principles listed in India's constitution. But under Prime Minister Modi, "the shadow of rightwing Hindu majoritarianism (or Hindutva) is ever present," Pratap Bhanu Mehta, a political analyst wrote in the *Financial Times*. Head of Ashoka University located near Delhi, he co-edited *The Oxford Handbook to the Indian Constitution*. He taught at Harvard and has a BA from Oxford and a Ph.D. from Princeton University.

Most Hindus Oppose Hindu Extremism

The manifesto of Prime Minister Narendra Modi's Bharatiya Janata Party "...seeks to redefine India's culture and institutions as inherently Hindu in nature, in contrast to the pluralist vision of the country's first leaders," notes *The Guardian*.

Most Hindus reject extremism and the attacks on Muslims. In 2017, six days after a Muslim teenager was killed on a train near Delhi, thousands gathered to protest the rise in lynching of Muslims and low-caste Hindus in Lucknow, Allahabad, Patna, Bangalore, Mumbai, New Delhi and other cities. Hindus, including prominent film actors, writers and artists, joined Sikhs, Christians and Muslims in the spontaneously organized protests.

Several notable Hindus have shown great courage in opposing Hindu extremism. Vijay Tendulkar, a playwright and filmmaker, wrote *Ghasiram Kotwal* (Ghasiram the policeman), a musical first performed in 1972. It satirizes the use of violence by a Hindu extremist party in Mumbai in the 1960's, to fuel its political rise. The play, a classic of modern Indian theater, has been performed over 6,000 times. In 1992, Sunil Gavaskar, one of India's greatest cricketers, walked out of his residential building in Mumbai and rescued a Muslim being attacked by a Hindu mob. This was during Hindu-Muslim clashes, triggered by the destruction of a mosque in Uttar Pradesh by Hindu extremists. Over 900 people were killed in the violence in Mumbai, most of them Muslims.

In January 2018 eight Hindu extremists, including two policemen, raped and killed an eight-year-old Muslim girl in Jammu & Kashmir. The police told the media that the accused wanted to terrorize and drive the Muslims out of the region. Two ministers in the state government, from Modi's party, organized rallies in support of the defendants. A human rights lawyer Deepika Thusoo Singh, a Kashmiri Hindu, is representing the victim's family. She was threatened with rape and death.

Virat Kohli, the captain of the Indian cricket team, spoke out against the rape. In a video, he asks "I have only one question if something like that happens God forbids to someone in your family, would you stand and watch or would you help?" Kohli is a Hindu with 26 million followers on Twitter. Over fifty former police chiefs, ambassadors and senior government officials signed a letter, which was sent to Prime Minister Modi, saying that the bestiality and barbarity of the rape and murder "shows the depths of depravity that we have sunk into...In post-Independence India, this is our darkest hour and we find the response of our government...inadequate and feeble."

Campaigning for a Temple, not Jobs

Modi's party says its campaign for the national elections in 2019 will be based on the slogan "good intention and right development." But the plan to get re-elected appears to be more focused on building a temple in Ayodhya, at the site of the mosque which was destroyed by Hindu extremists in 1992. The Indian Supreme Court will decide in 2018 whether or not to permit the construction of the temple. The opposition parties wanted the decision to be postponed till after the 2019 elections. They allege that the chief justice is a supporter of Modi who wants the court's decision to help him win re-election. Whatever the decision, Hindu extremists will launch nationwide rallies to celebrate or protest. Bloody clashes will likely erupt between Hindus and Muslims, as Hindu extremists try to win more Hindu votes for Modi's party.

An early test of the temple strategy was carried out during the election campaign to the Karnataka legislature. In February 2018, three months prior to the elections, a chariot march traveled through the state to raise public support for the building of the temple. It was organized by the Vishwa Hindu Parishad, a Hindu extremist group allied with Modi's party. A local leader of Modi's party is seen on a YouTube video telling a campaign rally that elections were not about good roads and drinking water. It was a war between Hindus and Muslims and electing the party that will build the temple. Modi's party won 104 of the 222 seats, its best performance in a southern state. Yet an alliance of parties opposed to Modi was able to form a government. It included the Congress party and parties representing a low-sub-caste and one of the two major Hindu farmer sub-castes in the state.

Jobs and College Quotas Split Hindu Voters

Modi's party is aggressively trying to prevent the formation of a similar opposition alliance of farmer and low-caste Hindus as well as Muslims for the 2019 national elections. The farmer and low-caste Hindus have traditionally opposed Modi's party, viewing it as representing upper-caste Brahmans and traders. Modi's party is raising the issues of building the temple and protecting cows to win Hindu votes. The party's upper-caste leaders are visiting low-caste homes and sitting on the floor to dine with the families. However such efforts to win more Hindu votes are regularly disrupted by violent upper-caste attacks on lower-castes and conflicts over caste-based quotas for government jobs and admissions to professional colleges.

The quotas for government jobs and professional college admissions are closely monitored by the political leaders of all four castes. The upper-castes, who compete for the few open seats, strongly oppose quotas for the low-and-backward-castes. Granting new quotas is also opposed by the low-castes, backward-castes and tribes, who fear it could result in their own quotas being reduced. To try to split Hindu voters who oppose Modi, state governments run by his party are saying they will modify some of the quotas. In the key electoral states of Uttar Pradesh and Bihar, the party's government is trying to cut the quotas for Yadav's, a Hindu sub-caste of dairy farmers. Yadav leaders are big opponents of Modi's party. (For a discussion of the caste-based quotas, caste politics and the strategy of Hindu extremists to win more Hindu votes by inciting Hindu-Muslim clashes see Appendix C.)

In 2015, while campaigning for his party in the Bihar

elections, Prime Minister Modi sought to rouse fears over loss of quotas as part of an anti-Muslim strategy. He said his opponents, if elected, will reserve 5% of the college and job seats in the state for Muslims, by reducing those for low-and backward-caste Hindus. An alliance of farmer sub-castes and low-caste Hindus, Muslims and the Congress Party won the election. Their government did not grant any jobs and college admission quotas to the Muslims.

Modi Elected Prime Minister with just 31% of Votes

Following the last national election in 2014, Narendra Modi was elected Prime Minister though his party got just 31% of the votes. This was the lowest percentage of votes gotten by a winning party in a national election in India. Yet Modi's party won over half the seats in parliament because the remaining 69% of the votes were split between two or more candidates from the opposition parties. In Indian elections, parties select candidates for each voting district. The candidate who gets a simple majority of votes wins the seat. The party, or alliance of parties, which win the majority of seats in the legislative body forms the government, irrespective of the share of votes.

Uttar Pradesh and Bihar are part of the northern states which form the Hindi-speaking belt. It accounts for two-fifths of India's population. Winning elections in the Hindi states require forming alliances between caste and religious parties to get the most votes in each parliamentary seat. Winning a majority of seats in India's parliament often requires, in addition, support from caste, religious and linguistic groups in the non-Hindi speaking states. Each of the states in Southern, Western and Eastern India have their own separate languages and scripts, culture, customs and food. Languages include Tamil in Tamil Nadu; Kannada in Karnataka; Malayalam in Kerala; Gujarati in Gujarat; Marathi in Maharashtra and Bengali in West Bengal. Some of these states have militant, right-wing parties representing linguistic-based interests.

Uttar Pradesh and Bihar, with the first and second largest population, account for a quarter of the seats in the Indian parliament. The voters in these two states hence play a major role in determining which party wins the national elections. In both these states the caste and religious demographics favor the parties opposing Modi. The Yadav's are Hindus who farm buffalos. They sell the animals to the Muslims, who run the beef slaughter-houses. The Muslims sell the buffalo skins to low-caste Hindus, who run tanneries and make leather goods. In addition to their dislike of the upper-castes, the Yadav's and low-castes oppose Modi's party for trying to curtail their dairy farming and leather business by closing beef abattoirs run by Muslims.

The economic links between these three groups make them natural political allies and their numbers give them enough votes to easily defeat Modi's party in the two states. In U.P., low-caste Hindus are about 21% of the state's population, half of them from sub-castes working in the leather and meat business; Yadav's are 9% and Muslims 19%. In the neighboring state of Bihar Yadav's are 11% of the population, low-caste Hindus 16% and Muslims 17%. In 2015, an alliance of parties representing these groups defeated Modi's party in the state elections in Bihar. This was a year after Modi won the national elections. Earlier in 2012, a similar coalition of parties defeated Modi's party in the elections in U.P.

In 2018, an alliance of Muslims and low-caste, Yadav's and another farmer sub-caste of Hindus defeated Prime Minister Modi's party in elections to four key national parliamentary seats. Three of them were in Uttar Pradesh and one in Bihar. One of the seats was vacated by the Hindu warrior-priest Yogi Adityanath, after Modi appointed him head of the U.P. government. Yogi had won the seat in the previous four elections. Another contest in U.P. was won by a Muslim woman, a candidate of the party representing the Jat farmer sub-castes. Ajit Singh, the leader of the party, earlier worked for 17 years as a software engineer at IBM in the U.S. A graduate of IIT Kharagpur, he has an M.S. from the Illinois Institute of Technology. Akhilesh Yadav, the leader of the Yadav party in U.P., has a Master's in environmental engineering from the university of Sydney, Australia. The fathers of both Singh and Yadav were the founding leaders of their respective caste-based parties.

The leaders of the Congress party and those of the low-caste and farmer-caste Hindus say they will continue with the alliance to defeat Modi's party in the 2019 national elections. Perhaps they will do so to win power, avoid political persecution, imprisonment or worse and due to popular pressure for a more secular, democratic India. But meanwhile, as an editorial in *The Economist* warned in 2017, "the fear is that, if the economy falters, Mr. Modi will try to maintain his popularity by stirring up communal passions. That, after all, is how his Bharatiya Janata Party first propelled itself to government in the 1990's."

Chapter 13

INDIANS HAVE TO BE MORE PHILANTHROPIC

Ian Grillot is a brave example of many Americans who welcome immigrants and oppose racism. In February 2017, the 24-year-old chased the gunman who shot Srinivas Kuchibhotla and another Indian engineer in a bar in Olathe, a suburb of Kansas City. The gunman, a U.S. Navy veteran, turned around and shot Grillot. A bullet sliced through Grillot's right hand and entered his chest, collapsing a lung and cracking bones. He survived. In March 2018, the gunman pleaded guilty in court and faces a sentence of life in prison.

An American takes a bullet, trying to protect Indians

"I still don't view myself as a hero," Grillot told the *Kansas City Star*. He said he was simply trying to do the right thing, to try to prevent the gunman from hurting anyone else. A White who served in the U.S. Marines, Grillot works in the home repair business. In April 2017, he was honored as an American hero at a festival organized by immigrants from 20 Asian countries, in the Olathe East High School auditorium. "The hate is silly. It doesn't really get us anywhere except broken hearts and heartache," Grillot told the crowd. More people of different colors and backgrounds need to stand up for each other, he added.

Grillot's mother told the *Star* that both her daughters would have also chased the gun-man, had they been in the bar that day. Since Grillot's courageous act, so many people have wanted to meet or interview him, have him give speeches or present him with awards that he felt like throwing his cellphone out of his truck window just to find peace, he joked with the *Star* reporter. "I'm vertical...I can fish. I am happy," Grillot said.

Indians joined Americans in raising over $300,000 to pay for Grillot's rehabilitation, through an online campaign started by one of his sisters. "Ian, You are an amazingly brave person. You have personified the real America, we all know and love. I wish you a speedy recovery and thank you, your parents and family for the values you have," Shailendra Singh, an Indian immigrant, commented on the crowd-funding site. Grillot also got a $100,000 donation from Indians in Houston, to help him buy a house. Both the donations got wide media attention in the U.S. and around the world. Philanthropic acts, of giving back to help others, generate a favorable attitude towards the donors and their ethnic group. As Grillot told the Indians who honored him in Houston, "I now have a very powerful message and if I can help empower people and spread hope and love, then why not?"

Indian Billionaires do not give back to Society

Indians are not generous in helping strangers in need or in donating time and money to help others who are less fortunate. India ranked 81 out of 139 countries on the World Giving Index 2017, far behind other developing countries. Indonesia, Kenya, Liberia and Thailand are ranked in the top 20 while the U.S. is number five. The rankings are prepared annually by the Charities Aid Foundation, a United Kingdom based philanthropy which manages over $3 billion for donors and charities.

A few wealthy Indians donate small amounts for social

climbing, business and political favors and religious causes. But only ten Indian billionaires, including three from America, have signed the Giving Pledge. There are over 140 Indian billionaires, including 121 in India, with net worth ranging from $1 billion to $40 billion, according to *Forbes*. The pledge is a public statement by the world's billionaires and their families to give most of their wealth to philanthropy. It was initiated by Warren Buffett, chief executive of Berkshire Hathaway, and Bill Gates, co-founder of Microsoft. Each individual donor decides the causes they want to support. The pledge is a purely voluntary act, with no scrutiny of whether or not it is fulfilled. The pledgers are mostly Americans, including the founders of Facebook, Netflix, Oracle and Airbnb. Americans believe it is important to learn, earn and return.

Buffett, 87, with an estimated net worth of $76 billion, has pledged to give more than 99% of his wealth to philanthropy during his lifetime or at death. He explains that he is not making any sacrifices by doing so and that he is being less charitable than most people who donate a bigger proportion of their incomes. "Measured by dollars, this commitment is large. In a comparative sense, though, many individuals give more to others every day. Millions of people who regularly contribute to churches, schools, and other organizations thereby relinquish the use of funds that would otherwise benefit their own families. The dollars these people drop into a collection plate or give to...(a charity) mean forgone movies, dinners out, or other personal pleasures. In contrast, my family and I will give up nothing we need or want by fulfilling this 99% pledge," Warren Buffett wrote on the Giving Pledge website.

Wealthy Indians rationalize their lack of giving by saying that the poor and less fortunate deserve no help because they are lazy and do not want to get educated and find work. Some Indian professionals in America also give little to charity. They say that they got into the top engineering, medical, science and other colleges in India and America, based on hard work and merit. Hence, they say, they owe nothing to India or America for their financial success. They choose to ignore the fact that the heavily-subsidized college education they got in India would have cost them at least $250,000 in the U.S. They also likely got grants and fellowships to study at American universities. So the minimum debt they owe Indian and American societies is the true cost of their good education.

Azim Premji, a Muslim and a Major Philanthropist

"I'm from an Indian family of professionals and my parents had to go through hardships themselves to send me to IIT-Mumbai. And having got the best of education myself, I firmly believe it is my personal obligation to give back to the community," Romesh Wadhwani told the *Economic Times*. He is an Indian-American billionaire who has signed the Giving Pledge. As for passing on all his wealth to his daughter, he says that children should only be given enough money wealth to keep them comfortable. "Leaving too much for one's children will take away their own entrepreneurial skills," he added. He is a founder of three successful companies.

In 2000, a "...deal - which was valued at a whopping $9 billion - gave me the financial freedom to do what I wanted. I wasn't interested in buying yachts; instead I wanted to carry on the entrepreneurial journey," Romesh Wadhwani told the *Economic Times*, discussing his sale of Aspect Development, a company he founded. "I set up the foundation early so that I could give it my best years and I plan to give away 80% of my net worth in my own lifetime," he added. He spends about a quarter of his time on philanthropic efforts. He contracted polio at age two and still has trouble walking.

Wadhwani has set up philanthropic foundations in India,

Kenya and other emerging markets to promote entrepreneurship and to provide skills training to high school graduates so that they can find high paying jobs. He also funds policy initiatives to accelerate economic development in Asia, Africa and Latin America. Wadhwani has set up research centers at the Indian Institute of Technology (IIT), Mumbai, at the National Center for Biological Sciences, Bangalore, and at the Indian School of Business, Hyderabad. He has also funded several research projects at the Center for Strategic & International Studies, Washington D.C. and the Indian Council for Research and International Economic Relations, Delhi.

There are some professionals turned entrepreneurs in India who are also making a positive impact on society through their philanthropic donations. The most prominent is Azim Premji, an engineering graduate from Stanford University. Founder of Wipro, a global IT services company, his net worth is estimated to be $18 billion. He was the first Indian to sign the Giving Pledge. His philanthropy was inspired by his mother, who tried to create "…a more humane, equitable and ethical society for all our citizens." She was a doctor who ran a free hospital for children with polio and cerebral palsy in Mumbai. "I was deeply influenced by (Mahatma) Gandhi's notion of holding one's wealth in trusteeship, to be used for the betterment of society and not as if one owned it," he states on the pledge website.

"I became convinced that markets, public systems and philanthropic initiatives all had a significant role to play if the country was to have inclusive development, and that we needed to work purposefully towards establishing a more humane, equitable and ethical society for all our citizens. I strongly believe that those of us, who are privileged to have wealth, should contribute significantly to try and create a better world for the millions who are far less privileged," he continues. Premji has donated over $5 billion, mainly to improve public schools in India, especially elementary schools. "Education is perhaps the most important social institution to empower individuals and shape a better society. And it's the Public Education System that does (and will) best serve the disadvantaged and deprived," states Premji on the Giving Pledge website.

"Having grown up in a middle class family in India, I was brought up by my parents to believe that wealth creation is about making a difference to society," says Kiran Mazumdar-Shaw, India's richest self-made woman with an estimated net worth of $2.1 billion. She founded Biocon, Asia's largest producer of insulin. Her philanthropy focuses on improving healthcare, especially in the developing countries. She is funding the use of telemedicine and technology to help improve services at several primary healthcare centers in rural India. She has also set up a 600 bed hospital in Bangalore, in partnership with a local surgeon, to provide affordable early detection and care of cancer patients. Mazumdar-Shaw has funded cancer research at the Bangalore hospital and at MIT. She says, on the Giving Pledge site, that "I would like to be remembered as someone who made a difference to global healthcare through affordable innovation."

Parsis as models for Philanthropy

It is in the self-interest of Indian billionaires and professionals in America to become major, active philanthropists, quite apart from any ethical considerations. They should seek to make a bigger social and political impact by coordinating their work through Indian associations and groups. Such actions will help spread a positive image that Indians are giving back to America and fellow Americans and not just interested in getting rich, buying large mansions and fancy cars. It will also help influence political, law enforcement and other officials more favorably towards protecting Indians from racial attacks.

Indians in America will benefit much if they follow the philanthropic example of the Parsis in India. They emigrated to India around the seventh century, to escape persecution in Iran for their Zoroastrian faith. They have the highest education levels among all religious groups and are very successful as professionals and in business. A tiny minority of about 61,000, most of them live in Mumbai.

The Parsis are widely respected in India for their major philanthropic contributions. The most notable work is that of the Tata family, whose companies are the biggest Parsi-owned businesses in India. For more than a hundred years, family foundations have set up and supported hospitals, medical and scientific research centers, sanitation, water purification, arts, education and other programs. Most of the funding comes from dividends on shares owned in the Tata group of companies. The trusts own a majority of the shares in the group, whose companies have a total market value of $145 billion.

Jamsetji Tata, the founder of the Tata group, set up the first foundation in 1892. He started funding top students for higher education because he believed "...what advances a nation or a community is...to lift up the best and the most gifted, so as to make them of the greatest service to the country." In 2012, in a document titled "The Tata Way," Ratan Tata, chairman of the group, noted, "We have to recognize that we cannot plonk ourselves in a community and operate in our own isolated way. We have to grasp the imperative of putting back into the community from which we gain riches."

Amar Bose's Major Gift to MIT

Like the Parsis in India, Indians in America should fund education, healthcare, job-training, civil liberties and other social programs. There are already a few major examples. Amar Bose has been the largest philanthropic donor among Indian-Americans and that too without attracting much publicity to his good work. Bose was an inventor who passed away in 2013 at the age of 83. He held numerous patents in acoustics, electronics and other fields, invented noise-cancelling headphones, the wave radio and an innovative suspension system for cars.

Bose Corp., the company he founded supplied high-quality speakers used in the Sistine Chapel in Italy, the Grand Mosque in Mecca and other public spaces and auditoriums as well as in homes and in Mercedes Benz, Porsche and other luxury cars. "I would have been fired a hundred times at a company run by M.B.A.'s," Bose told an interviewer from *Popular Science* magazine, in 2004. "Without character and integrity, you can make a lot of money, but I don't think you can be proud of it. I never went into business to make money. I went into business so that I could do interesting things that hadn't been done before," he added.

In 2011, Bose donated a majority of the shares in his company to the Massachusetts Institute of Technology (MIT). In 2017, Bose Corp. had $3.8 billion in revenues, according to *Forbes*. Based on the purchase price paid for a rival speaker company, Bose Corp. has a value of at least $4 billion. So Bose's donation to MIT is worth billions of dollars. Bose got his bachelor's, master's and Ph.D. from MIT, all in electrical engineering. He then taught there for 45 years. In the 1920's, Bose's father, Noni Gopal Bose escaped and fled to the United States. Noni was studying physics at Calcutta University when he was arrested and imprisoned for his opposition to British rule in India, according to an article in *The New York Times*. He married an American schoolteacher.

Bose's son Vanu Bose was also an inventor and patent holder. He founded a private company Vanu Inc. In 2017, after the American island of Puerto Rico was hit hard by a hurricane, the company provided over 40 cellular base stations to help with relief efforts, including searching for missing family members. Vanu got his master's and doctorate from MIT. He died in 2017 at age 52, from sudden pulmonary embolism. Like his father, Vanu was engaged in philanthropy, including serving on the board of the Boston Museum of Science. "My father would be very happy with the innovation and freedom of exploration that these grants have made possible, as it was exactly what he was all about," said Vanu in 2016, while announcing the latest group of recipients of the Bose Fellows Program at MIT. The fellowship provides faculty with funding of up to $500,000 for three years, to pursue bold research projects. "The awards acknowledge the spirit of insatiable curiosity that my father embraced," Vanu added.

In 2015, Chandrika and Ranjan Tandon donated $100 million to the New York University (NYU) school of engineering. It was renamed the Tandon School. Chandrika is vice-chair of NYU's board of trustees and is on the board of the Lincoln Center for Performing Arts. She founded Tandon Capital Associates, a New York based financial advisory firm. A Grammy award nominated musician, Chandrika is a graduate of Madras Christian College and the Indian Institute of Management, Ahmedabad. She is the sister of Indra Nooyi, chief executive of PepsiCo. Ranjan, a graduate of IIT Kanpur and the Harvard Business School, founded Libra Advisors. The family office was formerly a hedge fund, which traded in stocks, currencies and commodities. In 2012, Ranjan shut the $2 billion fund and returned money to outside investors, according to news reports.

Dinyar "Dinny" Devitre, a director of Altria Group, said that he didn't do much philanthropy during his career, but learned a lot from the American culture of giving. "You come to a stage in life that you have had your career...and instead of doing just business or making money, you want to give back," he told *Marketwatch,* a website that covers financial news. He added that Indians in America "...are looking back and realizing that they are doing well and feeling like, 'We owe India something.' " Devitre donates to Pratham, an education foundation in India, the Brooklyn Academy of Music and is a former director of the Asia Society in New York and the Lincoln Center for Performing Arts. From 2002 to 2008, he was the chief financial officer of Altria, with a market value of $125 billion. It sells Marlboro and other cigarettes, Copenhagen smokeless tobacco and wine in the U.S. Devitre got an MBA from the Indian Institute of Management, Ahmedabad, and a BA from St. Joseph's College, Darjeeling, India.

Community Actions to Counter Racial Hate

Indians in America will have to increase their work with community and political groups. "Working in our communities where we live is one of the more powerful things we can do," Prabhjot Singh told *CNN* in 2016. Three years earlier, Singh and a Sikh friend were assaulted by a group of boys and young men in New York City who shouted "Terrorist, Osama, get him." Singh lay on the ground waiting for the attackers to stop, when passers-by intervened and a nurse came to his aid. He suffered a broken jaw, dislodged teeth and other injuries. The two Sikhs were assaulted on a public street, hours after news of a violent attack by Islamic extremists in Nairobi, Kenya.

Singh is chair, department of health system design and global health, and a teacher at the medical college at the Mount Sinai Health System in New York. He got his MD from Cornell University and a Ph.D. in Neural and Genetic Systems from Rockefeller University. In 2012, after a gunman killed six at a Sikh Temple in Wisconsin, Singh denounced the attack in an opinion article in *The New York Times*.

"Shortly after I was attacked, I prepared to shift my work, to work in a community context, and learn how to be more rooted in the work of creating a more loving nation," Singh told *CNN*. "It's not easy, and I'm no expert. But if anything, being attacked primed me to listen more carefully and feel the consequences of our choices more deeply." His team is expanding the reach of a community health system. The goal is to improve the outcomes and decrease the costs of care for common diseases like depression, diabetes and hypertension in poor neighborhoods. Earlier, Singh was director of a New York social enterprise that sought to integrate data from personal health devices and from health care workers with information and payment systems.

Political Lobbying will Benefit Indian Americans

Indian Americans should fund lobbying groups and policy research to enhance their image among politicians, administrators, law enforcement and prosecutors. They should be able to collect large donations given their wealth. They can help elect lawmakers who will fight racism and support other Indian issues. At the top colleges, instead of opposing admissions of Blacks and Hispanics, they need to organize vocal alumni groups, make large donations and join the governing and advisory boards of the colleges. In addition, they should fund Indian student associations on campuses and monitor that Indian applicants are treated fairly.

In 2018, the Indian American Impact Project was set up to co-ordinate and leverage the efforts of philanthropists, politicians, community leaders and strategists to influence policy and help Indian Americans win political offices. Senators Cory Booker of New Jersey and Kamala Harris of California addressed an inaugural meeting of the lobbying group in Washington D.C. The political action committee was co-founded by Deepak Raj, a real estate developer, investor, former Merrill Lynch senior vice president, chairman of education non-profit Pratham USA and founder of the Raj center for Indian economics at Columbia University. Raj has a degree in electrical engineering from IIT Kanpur and an MBA from

Northeastern University. The other co-founder is Raj Goyle, former member of the Kansas State legislature. He is the co-chief executive of Bodhala, which uses technology to help companies optimize their legal costs. Goyle is a graduate of Duke and got his law degree from Harvard.

There are several American lawmakers and prosecutors who seek that Indians be treated fairly. Kevin Yoder is a Republican Congressman who represents the Kansas City suburbs where Srinivas Kuchibhotla was shot dead. In 2017, Yoder asked President Trump to condemn the killing "in no uncertain terms and send a powerful message that no American should be fearful in their own community. Diverse political and religious views are what make our country great." Yoder helped Srinivas' widow get a work visa when she was on the verge of being deported due to an expiring visa. In 2018, Yoder invited her to attend the President's annual State of the Union address to a joint session of Congress. In addition to supporting ethnic diversity, Yoder apparently realizes the value of the economic contribution of Indians in his district. There are roughly 15,000 engineers, math and science graduates from India working at the local offices of IBM, Oracle, Sprint, Garmin and other technology businesses.

In 2018, a prosecutor in Florida got a court to convict a man to eight months in prison for violating the federal Fair Housing Act. The man threatened to burn a neighboring house that an Indian family were planning to buy near Tampa. He was also ordered to pay $30,000 to Kaderbhai Ali Asgar, to cover the deposit he lost on the house. "We really feel that justice has been served, and probably this will be a deterrent to people who think that they can take the law into their hand," Asgar told the *Washington Post*. The hate crime against the chemical engineer from India occurred in November 2016, the *Post* noted, at the time of President Trump's campaign and election, with its racially and ethnically charged rhetoric and policy initiatives.

In 2018, Gurbir Grewal, a 44-year-old Indian-American, was appointed the Attorney General of New Jersey by Democratic Governor Phil Murphy. The state has the highest population density of Indians among all states. Growing up in New Jersey, "I was called so many variations of the (Nigger) word that it just confused me," Grewal said. He got a bachelor's from Georgetown University and a law degree from the College of William & Mary.

He was a lawyer in private practice at the time of the September 2001 terrorist attacks in America. Following the attacks, he was constantly harassed by a man who would wait outside the law office and shout "I've found him. I've found bin Laden!" Grewal told *The New York Times*. Enraged, embarrassed and tired of the taunting, He said he then made it his goal to get into the U.S. attorney's office, just so he could stand up in court "...looking the way I do and say 'I represent the United States.' "

"The American Dream is alive and well in New Jersey," Grewal said, after his nomination for attorney general was announced. He keeps a beard and wears a turban, in accordance with Sikh religious traditions. "I wanted to...show people that while I and others like me may look different and worship differently, we, too, are committed to this country...as someone who has experienced hate and intolerance firsthand throughout my life, I wanted to work to ensure that we all live in a fair and just society."

Chapter 14

A SHIFT IN INDIA'S BRAIN DRAIN

Up until 2017, many of India's top engineers, doctors and science, math and management graduates chose to pursue advanced degrees and jobs in America. This was because of reputed colleges, good prospects for finding work visas and superior financial rewards compared to those found in India as well as in Canada, Australia and the Middle East. But since Donald Trump became President, fewer American visas are being issued to Indians and Indian information technology (IT) companies, due to policy changes and restrictions imposed by his administration.

The Indian government has little economic clout to pressure Trump to withdraw his work visa policies. So it is quietly pushing geo-political strategies to try to gain some leverage. India is strengthening its ties with China, even as America is eager for India to ally with it against China. Prime Minister Narendra Modi and Chinese president Xi Jinping have held several meetings and declare that they have a close relationship. In the 1950's, before India and China fought a war in 1962, leaders of both countries spoke of a similar close friendship. Indian school children were taught to recite a slogan "Hindi-Chini Bhai Bhai" ("India and China are brothers.") In April 2018, the Indian media revived this slogan when Modi visited China for a series of meetings with Xi.

Modi is also encouraging Chinese companies to invest more in India. They are already providing capital and technology, including to mobile-based consumer businesses which face stiff competition from American companies. It appears Modi is thereby seeking to curtail the growing dominance of Google, Uber, Facebook, Amazon, Disney and other American digital and media companies in India. He cannot directly impose restrictions on these companies for fear of retaliation by President Trump.

Meanwhile Trump's work visa restrictions, along with sharp cuts in financial aid for advanced degrees at American universities, have helped answer some key questions for Indians. It is often asked what will it take for India's top engineers and other professionals to stay in the country, instead of emigrating to America? This issue is widely referred to as India's brain drain. And if they stayed, can the engineers build world-class technology companies in India, like they have done in America?

Recent graduates of the Indian Institutes of Technology (IIT) are not taking on $180,000 plus in bank loans to pursue Master's degrees at American universities. They fear they may lose their family homes since they are unlikely to find the high-paying foreign jobs required to repay the loans. Most IIT engineers are taking up jobs with large foreign companies operating in India, especially Google, Apple, Microsoft, Uber and other American companies. They are not keen on working for Indian-owned companies since the wages are far lower and there are limited prospects for career advancement and big financial rewards. They may soon emigrate to Canada in large numbers, despite the cold weather, since the prospects look very good. Or they may work for Chinese companies, at their offices in Southeast Asia or the Middle East or even in China.

IIT engineers, like other professionals, typically do not want to start a business. Only a few of them are willing to risk personal losses and career disruptions to pursue potentially lucrative financial rewards on their own. But as more top engineers stay on in India, some of them are starting their own enterprises.

The process is similar to what occurs in America, though the number of start-ups are far fewer in India due to constraints of capital, technology and talent. Since the 1980s, driven by both frustration and ambition, Indians in America have followed the example of Americans and founded businesses. While a small fraction of the Indians in America, they number in the thousands.

In India, the post-2010 wave of successful technology entrepreneurs are mostly benefitting from the rapid growth in mobile internet users. The start-ups are more numerous and in a wider range of businesses than the IT services outsourcing companies founded in the 1980's. Several recent start-ups are valued at over a billion dollars, ranging from the taxi-hailing service Ola to online retailer Flipkart. Both these companies were founded by engineers from IIT who had earlier worked for American companies in India. Their business success and wealth, after overcoming hurdles, will lead more professionals in India to risk starting a business.

The global success of American companies clearly shows the importance of hiring the best talent by offering superior financial rewards. More start-ups in India, as well as groups controlling the larger Indian companies, need to attract key employees by giving them bigger financial rewards, including part ownership, than those offered by American and other foreign companies. This will help them create big, global Indian competitors to the giant American and Chinese companies.

One potential for India is attracting mid-career Indian professionals from America. While financial rewards are high in America, the number of years during which most professionals earn their peak salary is at best a decade. American companies regularly sack employees, especially during recessions, due to constant pressure for higher revenue growth and profits. Most of those losing jobs are mid-career employees, in their 40's and 50's, since they cost more to a company to retain. While they may find jobs at another company, especially as the economy picks up, the jobs pay less and often last only a few years. Perhaps businesses in India can benefit by hiring middle-aged Indian-Americans professionals by paying them reasonable salaries. Many Indian-Americans will be happy to contribute to India, while they continue to be able to access their savings and homes in America.

India's top engineers and other highly-skilled talent will choose between emigrating to Canada, working for a Chinese company or working in India for an American or Indian company, based primarily on financial rewards and long-term career prospects. In addition, professionals seek a fair, merit-based system and laws that apply equally to all. Prime Minister Narendra Modi, or whoever replaces him if his party loses the 2019 election, should prosecute and jail business owners involved in fraud, not just managers and corrupt officials. The government should ensure that the assets of bankrupt companies do not end up owned by the same group that burdened them with large bank loans. These actions will help reduce future bad loan losses at the big government-owned banks, making it easier for them to make new business loans and fund economic growth.

The government should severely punish those lynching Muslims and low-castes and raping women. While this would advance human rights, it is also good for economic and national security reasons. India needs to attract more foreign investments as well as minimize the risk of radicalizing its 180 million Muslims. Anand Mahindra is the 62-year-old chairman of the $19 billion Mahindra Group of companies, including Tech Mahindra an IT company. In 2018, after news of the rape of two young girls, including the killing of an eight-year-old Muslim, he tweeted to his 8 million followers: "The job of executioner is not an aspirational job. But for the execution of brutal rapists & murderers of young girls I would volunteer unhesitatingly. I work hard to stay calm, but my blood boils over to see this happen in our country."

Appendix A

INDIANS IN AMERICANS PRISONS

The success of Indians in America has its dark side, including civil and criminal cases, fines and prison sentences. In 2018, Ramesh "Sunny" Balwani, former president of Theranos, its founder Elizabeth Holmes and the company were charged by the Securities and Exchange Commission "with raising more than $700 million from investors through an elaborate, years-long fraud" making false statements about the technology, business, and financial performance. The company claimed that its portable blood analyzer could conduct tests from a few drops of blood from finger pricks, revolutionizing the blood testing industry. Theranos' board of directors included Jim Mattis secretary of defense under President Trump, Henry Kissinger, the former secretary of state, and a couple of U.S. senators. Venture capitalists and the media hailed Holmes as the next Steve Jobs, the founder of Apple. Investors in Theranos included Betsy DeVos, secretary of education under Trump, and billionaires Rupert Murdoch, the media mogul, and Carlos Slim of Mexico. In 2015, Theranos was valued at $9 billion. This was before John Carreyrou started writing critical pieces about flaws in Theranos' technology for *The Wall Street Journal.*

A License Plate Honoring Karl Marx

Balwani emigrated to the U.S. from India in 1986 to study at the University of Texas, Austin. He has an MBA from the University of California, Berkeley. Earlier he worked as a software engineer at Lotus and Microsoft, according to *Crunchbase*. He then joined CommerceBid, an e-commerce company, which was sold in 2002 for about $230 million. Balwani reportedly made about $40 million from the sale. Balwani and Holmes were in a romantic relationship. He personally guaranteed a $12 million credit line to Theranos, according to Carreyrou's *Bad Blood: Secret and Lies in a Silicon Valley Start-up.* Scientists and engineers working at the company told Carreyrou that Balwani terrorized and traumatized them. Balwani drove a black Porsche with the license plate "DAZKPTL," apparently referring to "Das Capital" Karl Marx's book on capitalism.

While Theranos and its founder settled with the commission, Balwani is fighting the civil charges in court. In June 2018, prosecutors filed criminal fraud charges against Holmes, Balwani and Theranos. The prosecutor noted that "Silicon Valley, is at the center of modern technological innovation and entrepreneurial spirit; capital investment makes that possible. Investors large and small from around the world are attracted to Silicon Valley by its track record, its talent, and its promise. They are also attracted by the fact that behind the innovation and entrepreneurship are rules of law that require honesty, fair play, and transparency." According to his lawyer, Balwani did not defraud anybody and looked forward to defending his honor.

Carreyrou's book is being made into a film *Bad Blood* by Adam McKay, with an estimated $50 million budget. McKay was the director of *The Big Short,* a film about how a nerdy former medical student and fund manager made millions by anticipating the 2008-2009 collapse of the U.S. housing market. The actor who will play Balwani in the movie *Bad Blood* has apparently not yet been selected.

A Billionaire from Selling Opioid Drugs

In 2017, John Kapoor, 74, chairman, and six other executives of Insys Therapeutics were arrested by the Federal Bureau of Investigation. The charges allege that the executives conspired to bribe doctors to get them to prescribe Subsys, the company's cancer medication to non-cancer patients. The medication, popularly referred to as an opioid spray, is eighty times more potent than morphine. It was approved for use only to treat cancer patients with severe pain, according to *Forbes*. So far four doctors have been given jail sentences, ranging from two to 21 years, for taking bribes from Insys to prescribe its drug. They include a professor from the medical college at Brown University.

In the midst of a nationwide opioid epidemic that has reached crisis proportions, Kapoor and his company "...stand accused of bribing doctors to overprescribe a potent opioid and committing fraud on insurance companies solely for profit," a U.S. attorney stated. Kapoor was released on $1 million bail, pending trial slated to begin in 2019. He was the first person in his family to go to college and a got a Ph.D. in medicinal chemistry from the U.S. In 2016, *Forbes* estimated Kapoor's net worth to be $2.1 billion and placed him on the list of 400 Richest Americans. Much of Kapoor's wealth is based on his ownership of Insys' stock. It has fallen by over 80% since the FBI charges.

In November 2017, Rishi Shah, his co-founder and Outcome Health, the company they started, were sued by funds run by Google-parent Alphabet, Goldman Sachs and other investors. They are alleged to have presented fraudulent and false information to encourage the funds to make $487.5 million in investments, according to *The Chicago Tribune*. Chicago based

PASSAGE FROM INDIA TO AMERICA

Outcome Health places large touch screens in doctors' offices to display medical information and advertisements. Its motto is "Activate Good." The fund raising round in early 2017 valued Outcome at $5.5 billion. This led *Forbes* to place Shah, 31-year-old, on its list of Richest 400 Americans, with an estimated net worth of $3.6 billion.

The investors asked the court to award damages and also sought a return of their investment. A spokesman for Outcome told the *Tribune* that they see the lawsuit as a "money grab" that "simply is inexcusable and disappointing." About a month prior to the lawsuit, *The Wall Street Journal* reported that Outcome employees charged pharmaceutical companies for advertisements on more video screens than the company had installed. In 2018, Shah and his co-founder resigned from their operating positions in a settlement with the investors. They became chairman and vice chairman of the board. Shah, the son of a doctor, dropped out of Northwestern University to found a company which became Outcome, *Forbes* reported.

Victim of a Racial Investigation

In 2018, Raj Nair was forced to resign as president of Ford Motor's North American operations. This was after an internal investigation by Ford found "inappropriate behavior…inconsistent with the company's code of conduct," the company stated. Nair regretted that there were instances where "I have not exhibited leadership behaviors consistent with the principles" of Ford. Nair joined the company in 1987 and was earlier head of product development, chief technical officer and vice president of operations for the Asia Pacific region. He has a degree in mechanical engineering, specializing in autos, from Kettering University, Michigan.

In 2016, Sujit Chaudhry resigned as dean of the law school

at the University of California, Berkeley. This was after a woman employee filed a harassment lawsuit against him. Chaudhry sued the university for singling him out for further investigation because of his race, while ignoring allegations of sexual harassment against several other faculty members. The university agreed to pay $1.7 million to the employee and Chaudhry was allowed to continue his tenure as a professor at the law school, as part of a settlement.

In a letter to students, reprinted by a local publication, Chaudhry stated that "I have never been accused of any misconduct — sexual or otherwise — in my life before this case...My 11-year-old daughter learned about the lawsuit from the internet on her school computer. She read racist online comments about me that she cannot erase from her mind...I watched helplessly as my reputation as an academic administrator, a scholar, a husband, a father and a friend crumbled in a matter of days." Chaudhry earlier taught at New York University and the University of Toronto. A Rhodes scholar, he has law degrees from Oxford and Harvard Universities. He was born in New Delhi.

Crimes on Wall Street

The trial and conviction of Rajat Gupta was most widely publicized in both the American and Indian media. In 2012, he was sentenced to two years in jail and fined $5 million. This was for the illegal act of passing inside information, while he was a director of Goldman Sachs, to Raj Rajaratnam. The Sri Lankan born Rajaratnam was a hedge fund manager in New York. Gupta washed dishes in the prison and was punished twice with isolated confinement, according to news reports. He was the former head of McKinsey & Co., a consulting firm. He is a graduate of IIT, Delhi, and Harvard Business School.

In another case on Wall Street, in 2014 Mathew Martoma was sentenced to nine years in prison for his role in an insider stock trading scheme involving $275 million in illegal profits and avoided losses. Martoma also had to pay a penalty of $9.3 million, which was the bonus he made on the illegal gains, and forfeit his interest in a Florida home and several bank accounts. Martoma was an employee of SAC Capital. In 2014. the hedge fund pled guilty to fostering "pervasive insider trading." SAC paid a total fine of $1.8 billion and shut down the fund to outside investors. Martoma "traded his liberty, his name and his time with his family for what in the end is nothing," said Preet Bharara, the U.S. prosecutor supervising the case.

Martoma and his wife have three children. His parents moved to the U.S. from Kerala in the 1960s. He finished high school in Florida, where his father owned a laundry business. Martoma got an undergraduate degree from Duke University. He was expelled from Harvard Law School for forging one of his transcripts, in the hopes of getting a coveted clerkship with a federal judge. He then legally changed his name to Mathew Martoma from Ajai Mathew Thomas. He got an MBA from Stanford University, but the school later revoked his degree for making false statements on his application.

From 2014 to 2016, Navnoor Kang was a director and portfolio manager at the $185 billion New York State Common Retirement Fund. In 2016, he was arrested for allegedly steering "billions of dollars of business to broker-dealers who bribed him," the U.S. Attorney's office stated. The scheme involved paying Kang "bribes – in the form of entertainment, travel, lavish meals, prostitutes, nightclub bottle service, narcotics, tickets to sports games and other events, luxury gifts, and cash payments for strippers and Kang's personal expenses – in exchange for fixed-income business" from the fund, prosecutors stated. Such bribes totaled more than $100,000. Kang pleaded guilty to two charges and awaits a prison sentence, which could last up to 20 years. Kang earlier worked for Goldman Sachs and other major financial firms, according to his Linked-in profile. Born in India, he competed on the professional tennis circuit for three years. He was a graduate in economics from Columbia University.

Shivanand Maharaj was an outside business vendor to AFTRA Retirement Fund, a pension plan for actors based in New York City. Enrico Rubano was co-head of information technology for the fund. In 2017, both were arrested for allegedly fraudulently billing and pocketing $3.4 million in payments. The two "allegedly had the fund make payments based on hundreds of fake invoices to [Maharaj's] company, not for IT work actually done by that company, but really in exchange for alleged kickback payments to Rubano," the U.S. Attorney's office stated. Maharaj, an Indian-American, is free on bail, awaiting a court decision.

Illegal Payments to Politicians

Several Indians have been prosecuted for making illegal donations to politicians and parties. In 2014, Sant Singh Chatwal pleaded guilty to violating the Federal Election Act "by making more than $180,000 in federal campaign donations to three candidates through straw donors who were reimbursed, and to witness tampering," the U.S. Attorney's office in New York stated. "Chatwal then rolled the dice to stymie the government's investigation, thinking he could corruptly convince witnesses to his federal election crimes to stay silent. That gamble did not pay off," the U.S. prosecutor said.

Chatwal is a hotel and restaurant owner and a donor to political campaigns, including those of Bill and Hilary Clinton. As part of his guilty plea, Chatwal agreed to "forfeit $1 million to the United States." Though Chatwal faced over five years in prison, the judge gave him a lenient sentence: a fine of $500,000 and 1,000 hours of community service. Over 200 people, including self-help guru Deepak Chopra, wrote letters to the judge seeking that

Chatwal be pardoned. Commenting on the court decision *The New York Post* noted that Chatwal "appears to have retained a slew of friends in high places despite his fall from grace."

In 2014, Dinesh D'Souza pleaded guilty to illegal campaign contributions. It was "a bad idea. I regret breaking the law," he reportedly told the judge. Prosecutors argued that he be imprisoned for 10-to 16-months. He avoided jail, while being fined $30,000 and sentenced to five years of community service, including eight months in a confinement center. D'Souza is a conservative author and film maker. In a 2010 book "Roots of Rage," D'Souza argued that President Barack Obama is motivated largely by the "inherited rage" of his absent Kenyan father. Two years later he made a documentary "2016 Obama's America," painting a bleak future if Obama was re-elected president. The documentary is estimated to have earned over $33 million at the box office, while the book was a best seller, being popular among White conservatives.

D'Souza was president of the Evangelical Christian King's College in New York City. In 2012, he was criticized for reportedly being engaged to a woman while still being married to his wife of over 20 years. The news was reported by *World*, a Christian magazine. D'Souza was born in Mumbai and graduated from Dartmouth College. He raised the illegal funds for a Republican Party candidate who was a fellow student of Dartmouth. In 2018, President Trump pardoned D'Souza. While thanking Trump, D'Souza tweeted that the prosecutor Preet "Bharara and his goons bludgeoned him" to make the guilty plea.

A Self-Hating Indian?

D'Souza as well as Gupta, Martoma and Kang were prosecuted by a team led by Preetinder Singh "Preet" Bharara, the U.S. attorney for Southern New York. He was appointed by the

Democratic administration. Bharara was born in Punjab, India. He moved to America at the age of two, with his parents. He is a Harvard graduate and has a law degree from Columbia University. In 2017, President Trump fired him as a U.S. attorney. He then joined his brother Vinit Bharara's entertainment business and also launched a podcast on justice and fairness for public radio.

In 2013, Bharara's office arrested an Indian diplomat. In her application for a visa for a domestic worker hailing from India, the diplomat allegedly claimed she was paying the maid $9.75 per hour, while paying her only a third of that official minimum wage. After the arrest, Bharara was widely attacked in the Indian media as an "Uncle Tom," serving his White masters, and "a self-hating Indian." Some publications demanded that Bharara should never be allowed to enter India for insulting the diplomat.

A year later, in a speech to students graduating from Harvard Law School, Bharara said the criticism he faced in India was odd "since the victim was an Indian" and that the "white master" he served was President Barack Obama, who is Black. Borrowing a quote from a baseball coach, he told the students, "If you just go out there and try to be good, you have a chance to be great…Humility is important so you don't become unbearable…it will keep you open minded and striving to always do better…Self-doubt is my friend, and arrogance is my enemy."

Appendix B

STUNTED CHILDREN AND
FARMER SUICIDES

India has the largest number of stunted children in the world, according to a 2014 UNICEF report. About 47 million Indian children, including 38% of those below the age of five, were stunted due to chronic malnutrition. The problem becomes irreversible by age two. Stunting and other forms of under-nutrition are responsible for nearly half of all child deaths in India.

Stunting is linked to an underdeveloped brain and causes other long-lasting harm, including diminished mental ability and learning capacity and increased risk of diabetes, hypertension, obesity and other chronic diseases. About 70% of adolescent girls in India are anemic, according to UNICEF. Anemia impacts their future pregnancies and children. Stunting starts from pre-conception when an adolescent girl, who later becomes a mother, is undernourished and anemic. It worsens when infants' diets are poor and when sanitation and hygiene are inadequate.

A major part of the sanitation problem is defecation in fields, bushes and other spaces, rather than using a toilet. Around 40% of Indians defecate in the open, according to UNICEF. "Of the 1.7 million people worldwide who die from unsafe water, sanitation, and hygiene each year, more than 600,000 are in India," blogged Bill Gates, billionaire founder of the Bill and Melinda

Gates Foundation and co-founder of Microsoft. "A quarter of young girls there drop out of school because there's no decent toilet available. When you factor in the deaths, sickness, and lost opportunity, poor sanitation costs India more than $106 billion a year," Gates added.

In 2016, Prime Minister Narendra Modi began a campaign of giving de-worming tablets to about 270 million children, in an effort to counter infections and reduce stunting. The government has also spent $4 billion on building 50 million toilets and is pushing people to use them, instead of defecating in the open. By 2019, it plans to build 50 million more. "I can't think of another time when a national leader has broached such a sensitive topic so frankly and so publicly. Even better, Modi backed up his words with actions..." Gates notes.

The government also plans to provide free health care coverage to about 100 million poor families. The opposition parties have attacked the policy since only $300 million of the $1.9 billion expected cost has been funded. They say that it is aimed at boosting Modi's prospects in the 2019 national elections. While this may be so, wider health care coverage is much needed since most Indians have no medical insurance.

Poverty and Rising Inequality

"India suffers from having an environment that is inherently unequal," Ratan Tata said in an interview published by the Tata Trusts in 2016. He is chairman of the trusts and chairman emeritus of the Tata Group of companies. Roughly a third of Indians are poor, by the World Bank's definition of people living on less than $1.25 per day. Eighty percent live on less than $2.50 a day and 95% on less than five dollars a day.

About a third of Indians are illiterate, according to government statistics. The real number is far higher. In 2016, a survey by Pratham, an education charity, found that 58% of third grade students could not read at the first grade level. In the case of math studies, 73% of third grade students could not perform a simple two-digit subtraction. Government spending on education in India, especially at the elementary and high school levels, is very inadequate even when compared to similar spending by other emerging countries. In fiscal 2017, it was around 3.7% of GDP in India, while Brazil and South Africa spent nearly double that level.

At the other end of the economic ladder, "the share of national income accruing to the top 1% income earners is now at its highest level (22%) since the creation of the Indian Income tax in 1922," note Lucas Chancel and Thomas Piketty in a 2017 research paper. They add that "the wealth of the richest Indians reported in *Forbes'* India Rich List, amounted to less than 2% of National income in the 1990s, but increased substantially throughout the 2000s, reaching 10% in 2015." About 137,000 households, each with a net worth of about $4 million or higher, together owned about $2 trillion in assets, according to a 2015 study "Top of the Pyramid" by Kotak Mahindra, an Indian investment bank. These consumers are a small fraction of India's population but are sizeable in numbers. They are eagerly sought as consumers by global luxury brands like Burberry, Louis Vuitton, Gucci and Mercedes Benz.

Suicides by Farmers

Two thirds of Indians reside in rural areas, most of them dependent on agriculture. The inequality is equally stark in rural India. One percent of the farmland is owned by big farmers, each with over 25 acres. Many of them own land in excess of the legal limits by hiding ownership under other names. They use their political connections, being from farmer castes with large populations, to get access to irrigation, better prices for their produce and low-interest loans from government-run banks and farmer co-operatives. About a quarter of the farmland is owned by medium farmers, with farms between two and half and twenty five acres. Small farmers, with farms under two and a half acres, account for two thirds of the farmland in India. Small farmers have little or no access to irrigation, farm one crop a year and cannot afford to buy fertilizers and pesticides.

In 2017, while campaigning for the legislative elections in Uttar Pradesh, Prime Minister Modi promised his party would forgive bank loans owed by farmers in the state. After his party won, the state government ordered the government-owned banks to forgive $6 billion in loans owed by 21 million farmers. The Congress and other opposition parties want the government to forgive an additional $9 billion in farmer loans. They point out that the total loans owed by the farmers in the state is small compared to the $23 billion in loans owed by business groups to banks, which were forgiven by Modi's government. Farmers elsewhere in India are demanding that $40 billion of their loans be forgiven. In 2009, the Congress Party government forced the banks to forgive $10 billion in loans owed by 37 million farmers all across the country.

It is the big and some medium farmers who benefit from the loan forgiveness. Small farmers, as well as many medium farmers, do not have enough collateral to get loans from banks. Instead, they are forced to borrow from local money lenders to pay the dowries required to marry their daughters and to cover household expenses when crops fail. Loans from moneylenders carry very high interest rates and tough repayment terms. They are not part of the government's farmer loan forgiveness programs. Since 1995, over 300,000 farmers and farm workers in India have killed themselves due to financial distress from large debts owed to moneylenders, according to a report in *The Guardian*. About half of the 90 million farm households in India are in debt.

Inefficient Farming and Food Wastage

The farm economy, and the finances of most farmers, can be vastly improved with a few measures. In fiscal 2017, India produced 66 million tons of fruits and 128 million tons of vegetables. But a third of these food items is wasted, reducing the income of farmers as well as food supplies. Farmers are often forced to sell lettuce and other perishable vegetables to traders at less than a fifth of the price paid by an urban consumer. Also, while India is the world's second largest producer of vegetables, its exports account for only one percent of the global trade in the commodity. This is because India has less than a sixth of the number of refrigerated trucks and only 1% of the cold warehouses required to preserve fruits and vegetables, while they are being transported from the farm to consumers. Only 4% of India's food is moved through such a cold chain compared to 70% in the U.K., according a 2017 University of Birmingham report. Prime Minister Modi is providing incentives to private companies and farmer co-operatives in an effort to attract $15 billion in investments to expand India's cold chain.

In India, two fifths of the farms have some irrigation while the rest depend on the monsoon rains. Such dependence and inefficient farming amplifies the cyclical nature of the production and prices of farm crops as well as the quantity of food imports and exports. In fiscal years 2016 and 2017, for instance, the wheat harvest fell to an annual 87 million tons, from a previous peak of 95 million tons. The drop in output was due to lack of rains and extreme hot weather. So, in 2017, India imported four million tons of wheat. Meanwhile, exports of other food items fell to $15 billion that year, down from a peak of $39 billion in fiscal 2015.

Land use for farming is very high, due to population density and demand for food. About 390 million acres of land in India is cultivated, compared to 315 million acres in the U.S, though America is three times larger in size. The productivity of farms in India is very low, less than half that in the U.S. Most big farms in India are not large enough to use tractors, harvesters, sprinklers, satellite-based mapping systems and other farm equipment to increase productivity. In the U.S., where farming productivity is among the highest in the world, four percent of the farms – each over 4,000 acres - account for over half the farmland. Following the policy of the previous Congress Party government, Modi is encouraging farmers to lease their land to large contract manufacturers. The farmer is expected to earn a higher income from leasing his land than he does from farming it. Local subsidiaries of global food giants, such as Cargill, Unilever and PepsiCo as well as Indian companies, are seeking land to grow wheat, rice, corn, soybeans, peanuts, cotton, potatoes, tomatoes, cotton, barley and other crops.

Appendix C

THE POLITICS OF HINDU EXTREMISM
AND CASTE

Hinduism is the faith of 80% of Indians, while Muslims are about 15% of the country's population. For more than 3,000 years, the Hindus have been economically, socially and culturally divided into four castes. The Brahmans, or priests at the top of the hierarchy, served as advisers to kings and as bureaucrats under British colonial rule. But being few in number, they have very little clout in Indian politics. Since India's independence in 1947, they have advanced economically by pursuing higher education, relying on their long tradition of learning. The Vaishyas, or business-caste, control much of the trade and business. They are also few in numbers but have considerable political influence since they are big donors to parties.

The Kshatriyas, or farmer and warrior caste, are the largest in numbers, about half the Hindu population in some states. They are the major political force since the first national election in independent India in 1951. In some states, they have a unified identity, like the Marathas in Maharashtra. They typically vote as a block and hence dominate political power in a state. In other states, the farmer-caste is split into sub-castes, like the Jats and Yadav's in Uttar Pradesh. The sub-castes are large in numbers, often support different political parties and have a major influence in elections.

The leaders of the farmer caste and sub-castes have largely shaped national and state policies, especially in agriculture, education and government jobs, and brought major benefits to their caste.

The Dalits, or low-caste, are the second largest in number, about a fifth of the Hindu population. They are laborers whose jobs include cleaning toilets and sewers. "When people in America ask what it means to be from a low, untouchable caste, I explain that caste is like racism against blacks..." writes Sujatha Gidla in *Ants Among Elephants*, a widely praised book about her growing up as an untouchable, or low-caste, in India. "The untouchables, whose special role – whose hereditary duty – is to labor in the fields of others or to do the work that Hindu society considers filthy, are not allowed to live in the village at all...They are not allowed to enter temples. Not allowed to come near sources of drinking water used by other castes. Not allowed to eat sitting next to a caste Hindu or to use the same utensils...It was like this for me in Punjab, in Delhi, in Bombay, in Bangalore, in Madras, in Warangal, in Kanpur, in Calcutta," Gidla writes in her book. She works as a conductor on the New York City subway system. She is a graduate in physics from the National Institute of Technology, Warangal, India.

Hindu Extremists Praise Hitler

The Brahmans and the business-caste are the core supporters of the Bharatiya Janata Party (BJP), Prime Minister Narendra Modi's party. It is well-funded due to contributions from the business caste. Its leaders are current or former members of the Rashtriya Swayamsewak Sangh (RSS) (National Volunteer Organization.) The BJP is the political arm of the RSS being "ideologically captured and organizationally controlled by the RSS," Sudheendra Kulkarni wrote in *The Indian Express*. He was an adviser to Atal Bihari Vajpayee, the former Prime Minister who was from the BJP. Modi started his political career as a member of the RSS. In 2007, he wrote a book in Gujarati titled *"Beams of Light,"* about 16 men who inspired him, all members of the RSS.

The RSS is a secretive, Hindu fundamentalist, militant group whose core belief is that India is a "Hindu Rashtra," a nation of Hindus. Its ideology aims "...at ensuring the predominance of Hinduism in Indian society, politics, and culture, which it promotes through tactics that include violence and terror. Its agenda includes subjugating or driving out Muslims and Christians...," notes Paul Marshall in *Hinduism and Terror*, a paper for the Hudson Institute, a conservative Washington D.C. based policy group.

The RSS provides Modi's party with an organized, disciplined structure from the village to the national level. It has several million volunteers, organized hierarchically starting from a base of over 60,000 local units. The volunteers participate in regular military-based training programs. Carrying a wooden pole, they wear uniforms of khaki shorts, white shirts and black caps. The RSS seeks to extend its power and influence across wide parts of Indian society including through organizations for students, labor unions, intellectuals, teachers, industrialists, overseas Indians and retired army personnel. Its educational wing has over 20,000 institutes with over three million students. These schools distribute booklets to their students with maps depicting the "Indian Holy Land," which includes Pakistan, Bangladesh, Bhutan, Nepal, Tibet, and parts of Myanmar.

Early leaders of the RSS openly supported Adolf Hitler and Nazi rule in Germany. One of them M.S. Golwalkar wrote in a book, published in 1939, that "To keep up the purity of the nation and its culture, Germany shocked the world by her purging the country of Semitic races – the Jews. National pride at its highest has been manifested here. Germany has also shown how well-nigh impossible it is for races and cultures, having differences going to the root, to be assimilated into one united whole, a good lesson for us in Hindustan to learn and profit by."

Golwalkar and other RSS leaders attacked Mahatma Gandhi for supporting the Muslims. Gandhi lead India's non-violent struggle for independence from British and was a member of the Congress Party. The RSS and other Hindu extremists blamed Gandhi for splitting up "Mother India," following the partition of the South Asian subcontinent into India and Pakistan. Gandhi criticized the RSS for being " a communal organization," similar to Hitler's Nazis and Mussolini's fascists. In 1948, Gandhi was shot dead by a former member of the RSS. Gandhi's killing was part of a conspiracy by Hindu extremist leaders to destabilize "all efforts to uphold secularism in India," according to Dhirendra Jha and Krishna Jha in their 2012 book *Ayodhya – The Dark Night.* The authors note that the head priest of a Hindu temple was jailed for "exhorting Hindu militants to kill" Mahatma Gandhi, days before he was shot.

Hindu extremists continue to admire Hitler and the Nazis. They praise Hitler on online social media groups, buy Nazi posters and thousands of copies of Hitler's "Mein Kampf" in English and several Indian languages, notes Shrenik Rao, writing in the *Madras Courier.* In 2004, a high school textbook in Gujarat stated that "Hitler lent dignity and prestige to the German government. He adopted the policy of opposition towards the Jewish people and advocated the supremacy of the German race." The textbook was revised, Rao notes, when Modi was head of the Gujarat government. Rao is a Fellow at Oxford University's Reuters Institute for Journalism. Rao's 2017 article was also published by the Israeli paper *Haaretz.*

Destroying a Mosque to get Hindu Votes

Up until the mid-1970's, the leaders of the farmer and low-castes were members of the Congress Party or aligned with it. Their support, along with Muslim votes, enabled the party to win the national and most state elections. The party has been led by the Nehru family. Jawaharlal Nehru was the leader and India's first Prime Minster from 1947 till his death in 1964; his daughter Indira Gandhi was Prime Minister from 1966 to 1977 and from 1980 to 1984; and grandson Rajiv Gandhi was Prime Minister from 1984 to 1989. The party is now led by Nehru's great-grandson Rahul Gandhi. He studied at Harvard and Cambridge Universities.

For decades, Prime Minister Modi's Hindu nationalist party had little electoral success, given that it was supported by the Brahman and business castes who are few in numbers. In the 1971 national elections, for instance, an earlier incarnation of the party got just 7% of the votes. Since the 1980's, its leaders have aggressively sought wider support from Hindus by launching campaigns to turn Hindus against Muslims. They got the biggest impact from a bloody nationwide march to destroy a mosque and replace it with a Hindu temple. The mosque in Ayodhya, Uttar Pradesh (U.P.,) was built in the 16th-century.

A BJP leader told reporters the campaign was "...purely political in nature and had nothing to do with religion." In 1990, the BJP leader L.K. Advani rode a chariot from Gujarat to Uttar Pradesh, planning to destroy the mosque and build a temple. "I am sure it will translate into votes," he reportedly said. The chariot traveled through a large part of North India, covering about 6,000 miles. Along the way, Advani held rallies and collected bricks for the construction of the temple. The BJP and allied Hindu extremist groups mobilized large crowds for religious ceremonies to build the bricks from local soil, one each from over 200,000 villages. Prime Minister Narendra Modi, who was then a rising BJP leader in the state of Gujarat, was one of the key organizers of the chariot-led march.

When the chariot-led mob got to the mosque, they faced a

large police force who were under orders from the central government to shoot those trying to destroy the monument. The campaign and the chariot march led to over a hundred Hindu-Muslim clashes in various parts of India. Two years later, spurred on by the head priest of a militant Hindu supremacist temple, a mob tore down the mosque. The Uttar Pradesh government, run by Modi's party, reportedly backed the destruction. A 20,000 strong police force, sent to guard the mosque, vanished when the mob arrived.

The mosque's destruction was celebrated by Hindu extremists with fireworks and distribution of sweets in several cities and towns. It also led to Muslim protests and Hindu-Muslim clashes, in which over a thousand were killed, most of them Muslims. The central government in New Delhi, run by the Congress Party, removed the BJP government in Uttar Pradesh. A court order prevented the building of a temple. The march to destroy the mosque, the destruction of the mosque and the bloody clashes got the BJP new Hindu supporters. They were from the farmer and low-castes, who previously did not vote for the party. The party won elections in several states and got the largest number of seats in the 1998 national elections. It formed a government through a coalition with regional parties.

Web-based Images Spark Hindu-Muslim Clashes

Modi's party is campaigning to build a temple, at the site of the destroyed mosque, if it is re-elected in the 2019 national elections. The temple issue helps the party inflame Hindu-Muslim tensions as well as try to win Hindu votes in Uttar Pradesh (U.P.,) where the site is located. U.P. and neighboring Bihar are Hindi-speaking northern states which account for a quarter of the seats in the national parliament.

Hindu-Muslim clashes continue to occur regularly, largely

driven by Hindu extremists. Today the trigger can be opinions and images posted online, which are seen as major religious insults. In the pre-Internet days, clashes often started after the head of a cow was found in a temple or when the head of a pig was thrown into a mosque. There are cases where Muslim religious and political leaders, seeking to expand their influence among Muslims, have set off Hindu-Muslim clashes. Also, like the Hindu gangsters aligned with Hindu extremist groups, there are Muslim gangs who fuel clashes to expand their underworld empires. But clashes triggered by Muslims are few. They also suffer the most casualties and property damage. This is because they are far fewer in number and, more important, the police force is mostly made up of Hindus. The police openly support the attacking Hindu mobs, instead of protecting the Muslims, according to the findings of judicial inquiries into several Hindu-Muslim clashes.

Hindu extremists have also attacked Christians for allegedly converting Hindus to Christianity. Should Christians stop doing humanitarian work "for being so admired and loved that a stray beneficiary converts of his or her own accord?" wrote Julio Ribeiro in *The Indian Express,* following attacks on Christian churches and schools in Delhi in 2015. A Christian, he was the former head of police in Mumbai. "Is it coincidence or a well-thought-out plan that the ... targeting of a small and peaceful community should begin only after the BJP government of Narendra Modi came to power," Ribeiro added. In 1986, Ribeiro headed the police force protecting the Hindu minority in Punjab state from attacks by Sikh extremists. (See Appendix D for a discussion of this bloody Hindu Sikh conflict.)

Caste Divisions Among the Hindus

"Every day in an Indian newspaper you can read of an untouchable beaten or killed for wearing sandals, for riding a bicycle...your life is your caste, your caste is your life," writes Sujatha Gidla in *Ants Among Elephants.* In 2017, in Uttar Pradesh, under a government run by Prime Minister Narendra Modi's party, "Police harass non-vegetarian restaurants...but pay scant heed to incidents such as an attack in May by upper-caste Thakurs on low-caste Dalits that left one person dead and dozens of houses torched," *The Economist* commented. In 2014, upper-caste Hindu men committed over 47,000 crimes, including 744 murders and over 2,200 rapes against the low-castes. The real numbers were likely higher since many victims do not file police complaints for fear of further attacks.

While some low-caste voters may at times support the BJP, they typically support parties which promise to provide police and judicial protection from physical harm inflicted by the upper-castes. Hindu votes are also divided along caste lines due to the caste-based quotas for professional college admissions and government jobs. Since 1947, 15% of government jobs and seats at government-run medical, engineering and other professional colleges are reserved for the low-castes. An additional 7% of jobs and college admissions are reserved for tribal applicants. The size of the quotas represented the proportion of low-castes and tribes in the population. The justification was that the quotas would help these groups overcome centuries of discrimination.

The quotas were to be withdrawn in a few decades. But the low-caste and tribal leaders demanded their continuation. Also, neither the Congress Party nor Modi's party want to end the quotas for fear of losing the low-caste and tribal votes. In fact, due to political pressure the reservations have been expanded to cover other castes. In 1993, the central government set aside an additional 27% of jobs and college admissions for backward castes, mainly sub-castes of the farmer caste like the Yadav's. A majority of government jobs and admissions to government-run colleges are now reserved for various quotas. This is seen, for instance, in the admissions to the Mahatma Gandhi Institute of Medical Sciences in Maharashtra. In 2017, 69 of the 100 seats at the government-run medical college were reserved: 18 for backward-castes (sub-castes of farmers), 12 for low-castes, 7 for tribes and the rest for other caste and regional applicants. Only 31 seats at the medical college are open to applicants who do not qualify for the reserved seats, mainly the Brahman and business castes, Muslims and Christians.

Modi's party as well as the Congress Party have little room to accommodate more quotas, without angering the upper castes, farmer sub-castes and religious minorities not covered by the quotas. In 2016, the Jats in Haryana organized protests seeking job and college quotas. They are a farmer sub-caste, who are about a quarter of the population in Haryana and Uttar Pradesh. Modi's party had won the elections in Haryana – as well as the national elections in 2014 – with the support of the Jats. Yet the BJP government in Haryana was reluctant to grant the quotas for fear of losing votes from Hindus not covered by quotas. The army was brought in to clear violent protesters who blocked roads and tried to cut-off the water supply to Delhi. Thirty protesters were killed. The government gave in and granted backward-caste quotas to the Jats in the state: 10% in professional colleges and 6% in government jobs. It also gave $15,000 to the families of each of the protesters who were killed.

The BJP's appeasement of the Jats in Haryana will likely cost them votes from other Hindus in the state. This happened in Gujarat. In 2017, Modi's party won re-election in the state but with 49% of the votes. This was ten percent fewer than its share of votes in the state in the 2014 national elections. The party's majority was reduced to 99 out of 182 seats, down from 115. A coalition led by the Congress Party got 80 seats, its best performance in Modi's home state since 1985. A coalition of candidates representing farmer sub-castes, low-castes and Muslims was put together by the Congress Party chief Rahul Gandhi. He emerged as the leader of the political opposition to Prime Minister Narendra Modi, after the Gujarat election.

The Congress Party-led alliance got a boost due to votes from the Patels. This farmer sub-caste were big, early supporters of Modi. But their demands for job and college reservations were denied by the state government run by Modi's party. So in 2017, many of the Patels switched their votes to the Congress Party. Modi's campaign in the state once again focused on attacking the Muslims. He accused leaders of the Congress Party and Muslims in India of conspiring with Pakistan to hurt India. Modi's claim of a monopoly on patriotism and nationalism, political analyst Bhanu Pratap Mehta wrote in the *Indian Express,* marked "a new and dangerous low in Indian politics."

Appendix D

STATE OF EMERGENCY AND KILLING OF SIKHS UNDER CONGRESS PARTY RULE

The Congress Party has its own history of suppressing civil liberties and fueling religious clashes. In June 1975, a high court found Prime Minister Indira Gandhi guilty of corrupt practices in her 1971 election to Parliament. The court barred her from elective office for six years. She appealed to the Supreme Court to reverse the decision and continued in office. A few days later, she declared a State of Emergency claiming that non-violent protests against corruption were a threat to peace and the rule of law. The protests were led by Jayaprakash Narayan, a highly-respected independent social reformer. He started out as a young leader in Mahatma Gandhi's struggle for India's freedom from British rule. In August 1975, Prime Minister Gandhi got the national parliament to amend the electoral laws, thereby overturning her conviction by the court.

During the Emergency, Narayan and over 140,000 others were imprisoned without trial. They included 33 members of parliament, opposition and union leaders, teachers, journalists and students. Two students died due to police torture in prisons. Civil liberties were suspended and the media was banned from criticizing the government, the ruling Congress Party and its leaders. Censors sat in the offices of newspapers and magazines deciding what could be published. Sixteen high court judges, who opposed Emergency rules, were transferred in punishment.

In January 1977, Indira Gandhi lifted the State of Emergency and announced parliamentary elections. She was confident that her party would win. Leaders of the opposition parties feared being imprisoned again if Gandhi was re-elected. This fear and widespread public anger against the Congress Party pressured the opposition to unite. Parties ranging from left-wing socialists to an earlier incarnation of Prime Minister Narendra Modi's Hindu-nationalist party combined to form the Janata (People's) Party.

The party allied with regional parties to put up one candidate in each seat against the Congress Party candidate. The Congress Party got 33% of the votes but secured only 25% of the seats in parliament. This was its first defeat at the national level. Indira Gandhi lost the election in a seat which was held by her party for decades. The Janata Party won over half the seats, including all those in Uttar Pradesh and Bihar. During the emergency, several hundred men and women died in these two key electoral states, from forced and botched sterilizations. The program was conducted by the Congress Party government as part of its strategy to reduce the country's population. Voting for the parliamentary elections in 1977 provides a clear strategy to the opposition parties that, if they unite, they can defeat Prime Minister Narendra Modi's party in the 2019 elections.

The Killing of Sikhs in 1984

Congress Party governments have also appeased and promoted religious extremists. In 1988, for instance, India was the first country to ban the sale of Salman Rushdie's "The Satanic Verses." The then Congress government, pressured by Muslim religious and political leaders, said the book was an insult to Islam and the prophet Mohammed. The Muslim leader, who led the protests to get the book banned in India, admitted he had not read it. A year later, Ayatollah Khomeini of Iran issued a fatwa, or Islamic religious decree, seeking the death of Rushdie. The financial reward, to the person carrying out the decree, is still in place and is reportedly several million dollars. Rushdie is an Indian born Muslim who now lives in the United States.

In 1977, the Akali Dal, a party representing the Sikhs, had won the state elections in Punjab. The Congress Party, which ran the national government, sought to defeat the Dal in the state by splitting the Sikh votes. It funded and supported Jarnail Singh Bhindranwale as a rival leader of the Sikhs, according to Kuldip Nayar a noted investigative journalist. Bhindranwale was a minor, militant Sikh leader. As his support grew, he demanded an independent Sikh nation and incited violent attacks on Hindus. Fearing arrest, he and his group of armed followers took refuge in the Golden Temple in Amritsar. From within Sikhism's holiest shrine, he directed the killing of several prominent Hindus.

In June 1984, Prime Minister Indira Gandhi sent the army to clear out the Sikh militants from the temple. The army killed over 600 people, including Bhindranwale as well as innocent pilgrims. The bloodshed and the desecration of the temple angered the Sikhs. Four months later, the Prime Minister was shot dead by a Sikh bodyguard at her official residence in New Delhi. For days thereafter, Hindu mobs attacked Sikhs in Delhi, Punjab and elsewhere. The mobs were reportedly led by local Congress Party leaders. Over 3,000, mainly poor Sikhs, were killed in the ensuing violent clashes.

In June 1985, an Air India jet, on its way from Montreal to New Delhi, blew up over the Atlantic Ocean. All 329 passengers on the Boeing jumbo jet were killed. The Canadian police told the media that the plane was destroyed by Sikh terrorists. Thirty three years later, the official investigation is still ongoing and those guilty are yet to be identified. There is continuing tension between the

Indian and Canadian governments over the latter's support for Sikh groups in Canada, who are seeking a separate Sikh nation to be carved out from India. In February 2018, Canadian Prime Minister Justin Trudeau was ignored by senior Indian officials during his week-long visit to India. Sikhs in Canada, who number about 500,000, are big supporters of Trudeau's Liberal party. He appointed four Sikh ministers to his cabinet.

In 2017, Sikhs protested when Rahul Gandhi spoke at the University of California, Berkeley. The protest was organized by a group seeking justice for Sikhs killed in 1984. When asked about the protest, the Congress Party leader said "I am with them in their quest for justice...I lost...my grandmother to violence...Indira Gandhi's bodyguards, who shot her 32 times, were my friends. I used to play Badminton with them. So, on one day, I saw my grandmother shot and my friends shot. Violence against anybody is wrong, and I condemn it."

Acknowledgements

My writing this book was made easier by detailed comments from Charles de Souza, Mukul Pandya, Pranav Patel, Prashant Parikh and S. Ramanathan; also Harish Bhonsle, Bibu Bose, Cliff Brundage, Anna Chithelen, Joel Epstein, Shailaja Gupta, Vijay Karia, John Kim, Andy Lee, Dirk McDonnell, Manoj Mehra, Harald Paumgarten and Josh Weston.

I received generous support from Ajit Sanzgiri, David Cheung and especially Lyle Prescott.

I also want to thank Visakh Menon for the cover and Spencer Cheng for his technical support with the publishing. They help with Bryant Park Publishers, which I advise and co-founded.

The opinions expressed are mine; none of the above are responsible for them.

Most of the data in the book are from primary sources. The economic, industry, investment and other facts about India are from the Government's India Brand Equity Foundation. Over the years, and especially during the past two years, I have gained information and insights by informally discussing the issues in this book with dozens of American and Indian business executives, investment managers, entrepreneurs, policy makers, journalists, academics as well as Indian students in America.

www.ingramcontent.com/pod-product-compliance
Lightning Source LLC
Chambersburg PA
CBHW070929030426
42336CB00014BA/2595